Eating

My

Words

Other Books by Mimi Sheraton

THE SEDUCER'S COOKBOOK

CITY PORTRAITS

THE GERMAN COOKBOOK

VISIONS OF SUGARPLUMS

FROM MY MOTHER'S KITCHEN

IS SALAMI AND EGGS BETTER THAN SEX? (WITH ALAN KING)

MIMI SHERATON'S *NEW YORK TIMES* GUIDE TO NEW YORK

RESTAURANTS

MIMI SHERATON'S FAVORITE NEW YORK RESTAURANTS

NEW YORK'S BEST RESTAURANTS 1989

THE WHOLE WORLD LOVES CHICKEN SOUP

FOOD MARKETS OF THE WORLD (WITH NELLI SHEFFER)

THE BIALY EATERS: THE STORY OF A BREAD AND A LOST WORLD

As Historical Food Consultant

THE HORIZON COOKBOOK: AN ILLUSTRATED HISTORY OF

EATING AND DRINKING THROUGH THE AGES

WM
WILLIAM MORROW
An Imprint of HarperCollins*Publishers*

MIMI SHERATON

Eating My Words

An Appetite for Life

EATING MY WORDS. Copyright © 2004 by Mimi Sheraton. All rights reserved. Printed in the United States of America. No part of this book may be used or reproduced in any manner whatsoever without written permission except in the case of brief quotations embodied in critical articles and reviews. For information address HarperCollins Publishers Inc., 10 East 53rd Street, New York, NY 10022.

HarperCollins books may be purchased for educational, business, or sales promotional use. For information please write: Special Markets Department, HarperCollins Publishers Inc., 10 East 53rd Street, New York, NY 10022.

FIRST EDITION

Designed by Sarah Maya Gubkin

Printed on acid-free paper

Library of Congress Cataloging-in-Publication Data has been applied for.

ISBN 0-06-050109-X

04 05 06 07 08 WBC/RRD 10 9 8 7 6 5 4 3 2 1

To wonderful Richard Falcone, who has made work seem like play for forty-nine years and still counting . . .

With all of my love and gratitude

Contents

Acknowledgments

A S A WRITER WHO LOATHES WRITING and does it only to pay the piper for the life I love to lead, I have dozens of friends, family members and colleagues to thank for making this book possible, and there is no doubt in my mind where to begin.

Were it not for my editor, Harriet Bell, this book would never have been. Having previously guided me through *The Bialy Eaters*, this time she encouraged me and cheered me on through the darkest moments of doubts as she performed her incisive and sensitive editing. That we have now lived together through two books and still remain close friends is a tribute to her tact, her confidence and, most of all, to her patience with a writer whom editors have long considered a cliff-hanger on meeting deadlines. For all of this, "thank you" hardly seems enough.

Pat Adrian, the editorial director of the cookbook club The Good Cook, was the first to suggest that I write a memoir and she kept after me until I did. I hope she thinks that her efforts were worthwhile.

That the memoir came into being is due also to the diligence of my agent, Dan Green, to whom I owe much gratitude for his encouragement and his help in shaping this work with cogent editorial suggestions.

There are many people at my publisher, William Morrow, who also made my task easier and more effective, none more so than Lucy Baker, who provided valuable research for fact checking and took care of details that relieved me of much pressure. Because I have a fetish about handsome graphics, I especially appreciate the efforts of the design, production editorial and production team that included Roberto de Vicq de Cumptich, Ann Cahn, Karen Lumley, Sarah Gubkin and Leah Carlson-Stanisic. I also must thank Virginia McRae for making me look good with her impeccable and meticulous copy editing, always respecting my stylistic idiosyncrasies.

That my career became memoir-worthy at all is due to some great editors who had enough faith in me to train me and to trust me with marvelous assignments. Foremost among them is Clay Felker at *New York* magazine, who provided a showcase for writers, enabling us to do what we could not have done elsewhere, and for his two sterling editors, Byron Dobell and especially Judith Daniels, who first felt my work belonged in the magazine.

Despite arguments and harangues, it was exciting to work for A. M. "Abe" Rosenthal at the *New York Times* and with Joan Whitman, who guided me through my early years there, and with Marvin Siegel, a firm, insightful and good-naturedly insistent editor and an enduring good friend. I am also indebted to Allan M. Siegal for motivating me to find Otto, and also, later, for bringing me back to the *Times* as a freelancer years after I left.

Betsy Carter, first at *Esquire* and later at *Harper's Bazaar* and *New Woman,* was always generous with assignments and a joy to work for. Travel writing took on new dimensions for me when I was able to do so for Frank Zachary and the late Arnold Ehrlich at *Town & Country,* and both Henry Grunwald and Ray Cave were supportive of my projects at *Time*. No editor has been more helpful than Wayne Lawson at *Vanity Fair,* and none more fun to work for than Harry Evans at *Condé Nast Traveler.*

I also thank K. Dun Gifford and Sara Baer-Sinnott at the Oldways Preservation and Exchange Trust in Boston for inviting me to speak at their conferences in Apulia, Crete and Beijing.

Sustaining me throughout and forgiving my absences as I worked in my attic-dungeon was my dear and gorgeous family, including my extraordinary husband, Richard Falcone, our son,

Marc, our daughter-in-law, Caitlin Halligan, and our exquisite little granddaughter, Anna Christina Falcone, who is now beginning to express her food preferences, much to my joy and enlightenment. I owe you all many home-cooked meals and hours of babysitting, all of which will be my pleasure to provide. I also regret not being able to spend more time with my dear and ailing brother, Arthur Solomon, with whom I share so many memories of our parents, and am sorry that he and his wife, Lois, have lived so far away in Chicago.

Last but far from least, I must thank all of the great chefs and generous members of this country's food community who have provided me with inspiration and camaraderie. I share W. H. Auden's appreciation of your work as expressed in his poem "Moon Landing":

> Our apparatniks will continue making
> the usual squalid mess called History:
>   all we can pray for is that artists,
>   chefs and saints may still appear to blithe it.

Introduction—Fed Up

"**E**ATING AT HOME IS BORING!"

Any wife who spent time shopping and preparing dinner might be enraged by that pronouncement from her spouse. In this case, my husband and most valued eating companion, Richard Falcone, spoke my mind exactly, and much to my relief.

Having just left the *New York Times* after eight years as food and restaurant critic, I thought we were realizing our fantasy of the last two years—to dine at home, comfortably dressed, and perhaps indulge in seconds of dishes prepared exactly to our taste.

Dining at home also meant that I could cook to my heart's content in the dream kitchen that ironically had been installed in our Greenwich Village brownstone house just months before I under-took the job that would keep me in restaurants seven nights a week. (In 1983, my final full year at the *Times,* we had only six dinners at home, all on major holidays, one of which luckily coin-cided with Dick's birthday, when a home-cooked meal is a family must.) And so my state-of-the-art kitchen began to suggest a deserted mining town in Arizona; I expected to see the tumble-weed rolling in any day.

There we were at our own table for the fourth night in a row, and, as on the previous three evenings, I prepared the sort of sim-ple menu we had longed for. That night it was double-rib lamb chops broiled rare with a thin, charred burnishing of fat, crisp-skinned baked potatoes with fluffy white insides topped with sweet butter, coarse salt, black pepper and minced chives, creamed spinach with a hint of garlic and nutmeg, and for dessert, a ripe pear, shards of Parmesan and roasted walnuts.

It was not the food that bored us, but the venue. Although we both harbored that conclusion, until Dick's courageous outburst it seemed like treason to utter it. Perhaps there is truth to the old admonition that the cruelest fate is to be granted what we wish for. Finally, I admitted to myself what I had long feared: I was a restau-rant junkie.

If food is the main reason for my addiction, it is not the only one. Since childhood I had considered restaurants to be wondrous places. No matter what class of eatery my parents took me to, I had to clean up and change clothes, and en route in the car, I was reminded of manners. No wonder I considered the event special, as, in vastly different styles, we were greeted, seated and presented with menus, after which I could take the measure of my appetite.

Eventually I became carried away with the romantic notion of strangers gathering on the same premises primarily to satisfy the biological necessity for food, and, at the same time, socialize with family or friends, start a romance or end one, hire and fire, be hired or fired, wheel and deal, and always look good and happy to be alive, even if their world had just fallen apart. Meanwhile, on another level, menus are read, there are interactions with the staff, food arrives and is eaten, and the band of collateral human activity plays on.

As a child, I undoubtedly had an overly active imagination, fueled by the radio drama series *Grand Hotel*. I don't remember just how many rooms were said to be in that etherized hotel, but I do know the announcer promised "in every room a story."

I believe there is a story at every table. Anxious to know what each might be, I have honed skills at eavesdropping, glancing (too unobtrusively to be called staring, I trust) and filling in the blanks myself.

Food, of course, is really what it is all about. No matter how good a home cook may be—and my mother was an excellent one, as am I—there is an allure about professional finish, refinements, subtleties and variations. There is always the excitement, whether in a diner or a Ducasse, of seeing how close to perfection the kitchen will come with its own specialties.

What also appeals to me about restaurants is the luxury of returning a dish if it is not properly prepared, *because I am paying for it,* a circumstance that perhaps explains why some men, although happily married, visit prostitutes, home cooking and home sex having been declared vastly overrated by connoisseurs of both.

Most of all, because there were choices, I could retain my options as long as possible, something I value in all aspects of life. After selecting a restaurant, I do not have to make any other choices until the waiter's pencil is poised. I do not have to eat what others have, as at home, and, as I learned from my mother's examples, I do not even have to order it the house way. I cannot recall a single instance in a restaurant when my mother ordered a dish exactly as described on a menu. In one of his more perceptive monologues, Jackie Mason satirized Jews ordering food in restaurants, demanding that potatoes not be on the same plate with meat, asking for substitutions in vegetables, and meat that is rare but not too rare, lean but not too lean. I figure he overheard my mother more than once. Nowadays, as chefs' egos have souffléd, I have gotten arguments when I make such requests, and am told that the master will not make the switch (or serve sauce on the side, or cook to the degree of doneness I prefer), in which case, as far as I'm concerned, the master can eat it. Whose dinner is it, anyway? is rapidly becoming a burning question for serious restaurant goers. When critiquing, however, I always have it the chef's way, making a few special requests only to test the management's commitment to hospitality. Not for nothing are hotels and restaurants grouped as the hospitality industry, incredible as that may seem under many unfortunate circumstances.

Of course, Dick and I intended to go to restaurants after I left the *Times,* despite the sobering prospect of paying the check ourselves, a thought that could dampen any appetite used to sampling everything on an expense account. But on the night of our epiphany, we recognized that we were starved for the restaurant experience and we knew that from then on, we literally would be feeding a very expensive habit. We also became aware that we have higher quality conversations in restaurants than at home. It's as though we rise to the occasion by selecting worthwhile, less mundane subjects to discuss when eating out, just as we dress more carefully, even if casually. What came as a surprise when we began to dine out purely for pleasure was how much less pleasurable it felt when I was not reviewing, much like playing a game without the challenge of rules.

Even so, it became obvious that no matter how purposeless such focus and analysis might be, I could not suspend my critical faculties, and cannot to this day, whether the subject is a street corner hot dog or roasted squab at Jean-Georges' restaurant.

Given those longings and appreciations, one might think the job of restaurant critic would be an unmixed blessing and wonder why I gave it up. Life, however, is never simple, even when delightful and intriguing. As much as I adored this particular dream job and always felt a bit guilty about being paid to do it, so much was at stake for both restaurateurs and customers that I felt a constant and overwhelming pressure to be absolutely sure about every rating, even if it took eight or ten visits to a particular restaurant. That created a problem with my weight and limited my social and family relations, to say nothing of leisure time. The last straw was the unprecedented and intense pressure from a *Times* editor to change a restaurant rating (an occurrence to be enlarged upon in detail further along) and one that inspired me to go forth into the world and seek my fortune anew.

Difficult though that decision was, it was the only one open to me, despite the considerable plusses of foreign travel and friendships that developed as I searched out food around the world, not only in restaurants but in markets, on farms and in many types of production. And, because food is life, I gained insight into the lore, art, craft, psychology, spirituality and emotions surrounding the quest for daily bread.

I am always amazed at what I consider, for want of a better term, the human instinct for embellishment—whether of clothing, shelter or food. Those basic needs could be functionally satisfied with a lot less time and effort than we devote to them, were it not that few of us are content to admit that bread alone is enough. Or, if bread alone, then at least shaped into braids, crowns, starfish,

roses and pinecones, among other painstaking forms, that are classics in various regions, even though they provide no more nutrients
or flavor than if simply shaped into rounds or standard loaves.

The aspect of gastronomy that most intrigues me now is the philosophy of food—the ideas, humors and beliefs behind the myriad
food symbolisms in superstition, religion and folklore, and the
social attitudes that foster the rules of eating we call manners or etiquette. Two generations ago, children were admonished never to
eat while walking in the street, as it was vulgar. In Eastern Europe
bread and salt are considered lucky gifts for inhabitants of a new
home. In diverse parts of the world beans and carp are deemed
lucky and are required elements of New Year celebrations. After
many years of observing the eating habits of various dining companions, I feel I can tell a lot about someone by the way he or she
orders and reacts to food and then eats it, or not.

Although I covered many facets of food for *Seventeen*, the *Village Voice*, *Cue* and *New York* magazine before going to the *New
York Times*, and afterward *Time*, *Condé Nast Traveler* and *Vanity
Fair* among others, it was my stint as a restaurant critic for the
Times that even after two decades seems to fascinate audiences
wherever I speak on any subject. I may talk about the living drama
of food markets, the problems of institutional feeding in schools,
hospitals or airlines, how to judge the quality of chocolate or
caviar, the universal appeal of chicken soup, the agonies of picking
capers and why anyone bothers, or the tragic diaspora of Bialystok's Jews traced through their iconic bialy, but the first questions from the audience invariably are those that follow. I trust all
are answered in this book.

1. What is your favorite restaurant in the world? In New
   York?
2. What was it like to be at the *New York Times* and why did
   you leave?

3. How can one learn to be a restaurant critic and know about so many different cuisines?

4. Did you ever want to own a restaurant?

5. Did restaurant owners expect you in advance, and, if not, did they recognize you?

6. Did you pay for meals? If so, what name was on the credit card?

7. If a critic appears unexpectedly at a restaurant and is recognized, what can a chef do to improve food on short notice?

8. Were you ever pressured to give favorable reviews to advertisers or to the bosses' friends?

9. What do you look for when rating a restaurant? Do you factor in the tastes of others?

10. Were you ever sued, threatened or offered a bribe?

11. Did you ever have misgivings about a rating after the review appeared?

12. Are there any little finds you keep secret for yourself and do not write about?

13. What was the best meal of your life? And the worst?

14. Are there any foods you hate or are allergic to?

15. Are there any junk foods you like?

16. Does anyone ever invite you home to dinner?

17. Do you ever cook and are you good at it?

18. What changes have you noticed in food, restaurants and public taste in the fifty years that you have been writing?

19. How do you know if a dish is good?

20. What do you do about weight? (I gain it.)

The Making of a Critic

Like Mother, Like Daughter

"TODAY YOU'RE A MAVEN OF DRECK . . ."

"Good morning, Mother."

It is 8:10 A.M. and I know that my mother has been aching to talk since 6:30, when the *New York Times* arrives at her door. Unable to contain herself any longer after reading one of my most negative Friday restaurant reviews, she finally calls, certain that I will be awake.

"You think what you do is so nice?" she begins. "A man invests a lot of money and builds a beautiful restaurant and has a family to support. He has customers and everything is fine, until one day, in walks Big Mouth. Then you write and say that this was too salty, and that was too dry, and this was too that, and pretty soon nobody goes there. Who cares if people eat in a terrible place? If you don't like it, go someplace else. Do you think everyone knows what good is? And even if you're right, what business is it of yours?"

It would have been futile to explain that my business was exactly that, and, furthermore, that I was building a gratifying following. Just as pointless would be the information that I had won an award, or that I was told by several restaurant owners that they were able to get bank loans on the basis of my two-star rating.

I knew why the review had earned me the accolade maven of dreck—a connoisseur of crap in Yiddish. The subject was an Italian restaurant where I reported on the mussels, snails and eels I had eaten, foods my mother never would touch and so regarded as unfit for all humans. It was a strange line in the sand drawn by a woman who not only ate but prepared raw and cooked clams and oysters, every kind of fish, innards like brains, sweetbreads, heart, liver, kidneys and lungs and who, when making pickled herring, mashed the spleen (miltz) to add creaminess to the brine.

"We don't eat mussels, snails and eels," she said. By "we," I knew she meant Jews.

"I don't know about we," I answered, "but you haven't a kosher bone in your body and the we you're talking about don't eat clams or oysters, either. You also say we don't eat olive oil, but that will be news to Sephardic Jews and many Israelis. So who are we?"

"A sane person can't talk to you. You'd better speak to your father."

Many readers of my *Times* columns shared my mother's opinion of me as nitpicker and busybody, questioning not only my aesthetic judgments but my morals and my sanity. Among such was a Brooklyn minister who wrote, "If Mimi Sheraton were invited to dinner beyond the Pearly Gates, she would probably complain that the light was too bright." To which I replied, "If it were, I would."

When I described a tiny, succulent soft-shell crab as looking like an infant's hand, a reader warned the editors, "Be careful. Your critic is becoming cannibalistic."

Similarly, in a review of a very authentic Japanese restaurant, I reported on first being shocked to see lobster sashimi presented as a split lobster, still energetically writhing on my plate. Recovering quickly, I dug in and so was able to praise the meat's silken texture and airy, sea-breeze flavor.

"Your restaurant critic has lost her mind," came the first of several irate letters. "She is now eating live animals."

My answer now, as then, is that it is arguable whether any creature that has been cut in half is really alive just because nerves are twitching. Or to point out that devotees of clams and oysters on the half shell better be eating them live if the eaters want to stay that way. Perhaps bivalve mollusks arouse little sympathy because they have less personality than crustaceans and their stubborn fight for life is apparent only to shuckers. In any event, I assured readers that even I had humanitarian limits, citing my refusal of a dinner invitation in Hong Kong in 1960, when the special treat was to be monkey brains, served as a dip in the chopped-open head still attached to the live—or, at least, quivering—animal.

One of my most persistent critics through the years sent postcards to the *Times*, sometimes addressed to me by name, other times only to "Maven af Pork Ass," a sobriquet that did not stump the mail-room staff at all. Whether neatly typed or handwritten in a wild sprawl, these picture postcards came from various restaurants whenever I reported on eating pork. Each was signed with a different female name, once that of the legendary actress Molly Picon. Having obviously read me for some time, the writer knew that my grandfather had been a rabbi, who, I was warned, must be

turning in his grave. I was admonished to think more about my
ancestral heritage and less about pork ass, and was advised, as a
parting thought, "You have too much to say in general, anyway."
My mother couldn't have said it any better.

Although my parents were proud of my working at the *New York
Times,* they hated my role as a restaurant critic, my father mainly
because he feared I might be harmed by an irate owner. Fortunately,
he needn't have worried. I was never even threatened, no less
harmed, nor was I ever offered a bribe. My mother, although my
fiercest defender, expressed her unconditional love through unre-
lenting criticism that she clearly meant to be constructive—for my
own good. And not only with food. In summer, she said my dress
looked too warm. In winter, she said my coat did not look warm
enough. When I told her I was taking a second trip to Europe, she
advised, "Take a really good look this time, so you don't have to go
back again!" And when I had my apartment walls painted white, she
chided, "For the same money, you could have a color!"

When I finally began writing about food and recipes, she tended
to argue about any ingredients she herself would not use, or any
combination she thought bizarre, no matter how classic. When she
watched me cook she became a combination director and efficiency
expert, nudging me to handle food and utensils with authority.
"Don't be afraid of it," she would yell. "Remember you're the boss
of the food. Don't *kitsel* it!" I especially recall her berating me once
as I was chopping chicken livers and, in her view, lifting the half-
moon chopper too high out of the wooden bowl, thereby wasting
time and energy in thrusting it down farther than I had to. "Take
shorter strokes! The liver will be chopped just as fine, and faster.
It's how many times you chop down, not how high you go in
between," she admonished. If Frederick Taylor was the father of
the time-motion study, she surely was the mother.

Never mind that I already had completed courses at the Cordon

Bleu in Paris and written two cookbooks and that she always enjoyed the food I prepared. If she watched, she wanted it done her way. Using the same utensils, I still automatically chop to the rhythmic mantra "take-shorter-strokes."

What started us cooking together many years after I left home was a collection of her recipes for a memoir-cookbook *From My Mother's Kitchen*, first published in 1979. Before that, I had recorded some of her recipes, but I realized time might run out before I had them all. A book contract would mean a deadline and force me to gather everything that might otherwise be lost. But because my mother was an old-fashioned cook who measured ingredients only when baking, I knew that to get things right, I would have to watch her prepare the dishes and slip measuring spoons and cups under her, so to speak.

Not surprisingly, it drove her crazy. "Are we going to measure, or are we going to cook?" she asked in desperation, begging me to quit the project and even offering to pay me to do so.

"How much?" I asked.

She considered for a minute, then obviously went for broke. "Fifty dollars," she answered, indicating her estimate of my worth in the publishing marketplace. Although my mother generally approved of my articles on judging quality in food products, she was hardly intimidated by my expertise, even when I told her that a garlicky kielbasa that I had recommended at J. Kurowycky & Sons in New York's East Village drew 127 people to the shop by 8:30 A.M. Nor was she impressed when the great French pâtissière Maurice Bonté reported that after my article praising the ladyfingers at his bakery, they accounted for one-third of all sales for the next five years. Despite such reader confidence, I don't think I ever bought a pound of ground beef or a bunch of carrots for my mother that she deemed wholly perfect. Nor did my father, who dealt in wholesale fruits and vegetables in the bygone Washington Market.

"That's the head of lettuce a man in the produce business brings home?" she typically would comment on his selection.

Her constant dissatisfaction was an involuntary reflex and probably genetic, inherited from her mother and shared by her four sisters, although I don't know if this trait extended to her four brothers. It was hard to live with but proved excellent discipline for someone who would grow up to write about food and search for the best.

The toughest taskmaster was Grandma Breit, an indefatigable, nagging mother of nine who was a wonderful cook, devoutly kosher and perpetually in need of something from the store. In her later years she lived alone just a block away from us, and because she had trouble walking, could not shop for herself and so relied on the telephone and her family. With a chair pulled close to her kitchen window on the ground floor, she was ever on the alert for a grandchild to dispatch. Hating such errands, I used to hug the building as I walked by so that I could crouch undiscovered beneath her window ledge. Sometimes she leaned out for a breath of air and I was caught.

The specs she issued were precise: color, texture, degrees of fat, the brown mottling that indicated a grapefruit would be sweet, the thin-skinned lemons that would be easier to squeeze. If it were even as little as one-eighth pound (a.k.a. a half-from-a-quarter) of lox, two water bagels or a slice of calf's liver, I was told to say it was for Mrs. Breit. Being painfully shy and having been teased by some customers at the butcher shop once when I uttered that warning, I never did so again. And each time my grandmother unwrapped a package she examined the contents and accused, "You didn't say it was for Mrs. Breit!"

How could she have known? What flaw gave me away? Had she called the storekeeper to ask if I'd uttered the magic words?

Like mother, like daughter, and so with my mother, who also always needed something no matter how much she had ordered or how many times she sent me or my brother to the store. I found it so annoying and intrusive to be tethered to an assignment when I wanted to take a nonobjective walk that I vowed never to be that way. Even now when I am cooking and Dick goes out asking if I need anything, I say no. The answer almost kills me for, in truth, I, too, always do need something, but I refuse to break my pact even if it is only with myself. At such times, I could swear I hear my mother's whispery cigarette voice: "Don't be a fool. Tell him to bring something back even if it's only a can of tomatoes that you don't need now. It's good training, the tomatoes will keep and you have control even while he is out."

It is Sunday morning and Dick, our five-year-old son, Marc, and I are driving over to Brooklyn to spend the afternoon with my parents.

"Can I bring you anything?" I call and ask before leaving home.

"Well, if I had a chicken, I'd make a plate of soup," my mother answers.

"Fine. I'll buy a chicken and soup greens, too," I offer.

"*You'll* buy a chicken?" she asks as though I had suggested flying to the moon under my own power.

"Yes, Mother. I'm a college graduate and I majored in buying chickens."

"Fresh mouth! Where will you buy it?"

"Balducci's."

"It won't be a Jewish chicken."

"No. But on the ride over we'll say a few *broche*s and by the time we get to Brooklyn, it'll be Jewish."

Again, although not kosher, my mother liked a Jewish chicken for soup and Jewish fish for gefilte fish. If you think it's hard to tell if a chicken is Jewish, just try detecting that in a carp, unless, of course, it speaks Hebrew as one was reported to have done recently in a Hasidic community in Upper New York State.

And so we get to my parents' apartment and I hand my mother the shopping bag and disappear into the living room. That way I avoid seeing her expression as she scrutinizes the chicken and greens. Dick settles down in front of the television set to watch Sunday football, thus insulating himself from the general proceedings. Marc cavorts with my father, tying him in a chair as usual. I sit at the grand piano and play the first five bars of Brahms's Hungarian Dance no. 5, almost the sum total of my musical abilities after seven years of piano lessons.

I am determined not to ask about the chicken, but I listen. I hear paper tearing as the bag is opened, then water running as the chicken is being washed. The top of the glass salt jar clicks against the bottom as the chicken is being salted. A platter clinks as it is slid off the shelf, and then the door to the refrigerator opens and shuts.

Still no comment from the kitchen. I blink first and call out, "How's the chicken, Ma?"

After a pinpoint pause of hesitation, I hear, "Oh . . . It's going to be fine, darling. Thank you very much for bringing it. I know how busy you must be."

Before leaving, we have a delicious afternoon meal, with vanilla- and cinnamon-scented cheese blintzes all hot and buttery under a cool mantle of sour cream, and nut-strewn yeast cake to go with dark, strong coffee.

My mother and I spoke almost every day, and after about a week, when the chicken episode was barely a memory, she seized an opening in our rambling conversation.

"Now! First, don't feel badly, but you should know there was no petrouchka [parsley root] in with the greens, so the soup didn't have that nice sweet taste. Then I want to tell you how to pick out a really good soup chicken, Mrs. Gourmet!" By really good, she meant a nice big, fat, yellow fowl (for which a special order is necessary at most markets), one with a slightly pliable breastbone, and, if she had her way, purchased at a live poultry market where one can blow feathers apart to judge skin and fat, and test beak and feet for flexibility.

If my parents were unhappy about my work, they had only themselves to blame, for in addition to all of the shopping exercises, there was the ritual discussion of the food served at every meal. So whenever I am asked, "How can I become a food critic like you?" I am always tempted to answer, "Live my life." Start by having Beatrice Breit Solomon and Joseph Solomon as sociable, fairly assimilated middle-class Jewish parents and Arthur Solomon as a kid brother, and though it does not require growing up in a small private house on a tree-lined street in the Midwood section of Flatbush, it couldn't hurt.

As we each recounted our day's activities at dinner, my father not only explained the problems, falling prices and risks of rotting perishables he dealt with as a wholesaler, but also of the products he handled each day and the plans for next season's merchandise—which crops he would contract for in Texas, which in Georgia, and so on. Thus was it repeated constantly that California oranges were far more flavorful than their juicier but sweetly bland Florida cousins, but that grapefruit from Florida's Indian River had more pungency and character. As for apples, those from Washington State were (and are) pulpy, candy-sweet impostors compared to the icy crackle of tangy varieties such as Macouns and McIntoshes from Massachusetts and New York, where early night frosts imparted character to the fruit. And so on, with kudos for New Jersey's tomatoes because they were less watery than Long Island's,

and if peaches didn't come from Georgia, why buy them? But the
biggest tomfoolery in his eyes was the high value placed on size and
appearance over flavor and texture, most especially in the fruits
destined for costly gift baskets. "Food is to eat, not to look at," was
one of his mottoes that I think of often when facing some of the
overarranged plates so fashionable today. Although I was unaware
of it, such table talk taught me that nature still plays a part in deter-
mining the quality and characteristics of fruits, vegetables, seafood,
meats, grains and other foods, and so careful discernment is necessary in evaluating products of different varieties and regions. Only
tasting is believing. Inadvertently, I learned to focus on flavors and
commit them to memory so that I could understand and take part in
the discussions.

My mother was an ambitious and gifted cook who had open
contempt for any woman who was not. "That woman can't even
make a decent plate of chicken soup" relegated the unfortunate
subject to the bottom of her social list—someone capable of God-
knows-what and certainly unfit to marry anyone in our extended
family of uncles and eight male cousins, which usually was the
point. I counted on finding my mother in the kitchen whenever I
wanted to see her, or did my homework on the big table, where she
would sustain me with tempting morsels. That way I caught sub-
liminal glimpses of how certain foods looked and were handled in
stages of preparation: meat not too tightly packed for hamburgers,
breaded cutlets allowed to dry on a rack before being fried, and just
the right supple, almost fabric-like texture for piecrust dough as it
draped over the rolling pin.

Understandably, my mother liked to be praised for her cooking,
and if no one else complied, she did the honors herself, announcing how good everything was or how she intended to change it next
time. Insulted if we did not like a dish one time so much as we had

before, she would tighten her lips and promise, "This is the way I am going to make it from now on." But, of course, she reverted to the version we preferred, for she, like most cooks, was generous and wanted to please. She invited discussion. Was it too salty? Was it too dry? Too well done? Too rare? Was it too this or that? It's a wonder she didn't recognize such critiques in my reviews as being echoes of those she had encouraged.

Thinking back, I realize how little I know about my parents' personalities and ambitions before I was born. If I could have an answer to only one telling question it would be: "How come you two did not observe rules of kashruth?"

I knew that they never had, even at the beginning of their marriage, an indication, I've always hoped, that they had been rebels. How else to account for the fact that having both been raised in ultra-Orthodox homes with my mother's parents every bit as religious as my paternal grandfather, who was a rabbi, they opted out of dietary laws entirely? They were not even disturbed when their parents would not eat at our home unless it was an all-dairy meal served on paper plates with disposable utensils. Perhaps it was part of first-generation assimilation, as they had been brought up in the Williamsburg section of Brooklyn, where my mother was born, and to which my father was brought as an infant. My mother's parents emigrated from southern Poland—Galicia—and my father's from Germany and western Poland, first stopping in London, where my grandfather presided over a synagogue in Whitechapel, housing his family in the basement, where my father was born.

They observed other aspects of Judaism in their own ways, celebrating major holidays but not minor, founding an Orthodox synagogue but not observing the Sabbath and not being kosher, choosing freely among rituals in much the same way they ordered from a Chinese menu—one choice from A, two from B, nothing from C, thank you. But it remains a mystery as to when and how they first ventured into eating their much loved shellfish, bacon and ham and combining dairy with meat, and developed into a couple unable to get within two blocks of a clam bar without bellying up for a dozen each. My mother supplemented her Eastern European Jewish dishes with a wide repertory of American recipes from newspaper clippings: lobster Newburg, shrimp creole, her take on subgum chow mein, creamed chicken à la king in puff-pastry patty shells, and more, especially for ladies' lunches and midnight suppers after card games.

Above all, my parents loved going to restaurants, a habit they probably developed during the first nine years of their marriage, when they prospered but had no children. In addition, working in an ethnically mixed business, my father had lunch daily with Jews, Italians, Irish and Germans. Old-time menus in the handsome bar-and-grill taverns formerly in the market area that is now the trendy TriBeCa featured oysters on the half shell, Yankee bean soup, London broil with mushroom gravy, corned beef and cabbage, sauerbraten with potato pancakes, calf's liver and bacon and seasonal favorites such as soft-shell crabs, smelts and whitebait with oyster crabs.

And my father had his own way of ordering. Not for him the standard blue-plates or garnishes described on the menu. I loved having lunch at one of those seductively macho places with their black- and white-tiled floors, etched mirrors and dark wood paneling when a weekday school holiday left me free to spend the day in his office. If there were fried soft-shell crabs, he would say, "Just bring a big platter with about a dozen or so and never mind the green stuff . . ." Despite his occupation, he hated most of the green stuff—vegetables. At home he would say to my mother in Yiddish (so my brother and I would not understand), "*Nisht kein griner.*" Needless to say, it didn't take long for us to figure out the meaning of that phrase and to repeat it in Yiddish as a sort of family joke, whenever lima beans, peas, turnips or Brussels sprouts were in view.

Perhaps because I was an only child for seven and a half years before my brother, Arthur, was born, I was taken to many restaurants for anniversary and birthday celebrations, not only for shore dinners at the legendary, original Lundy's, then on a pier jutting into Sheepshead Bay, but to a bygone Manhattan steakhouse, Fan & Bill's. There I was bowled over by the gigantic plank steak, a colorful classic of the times. In the middle of a huge oval oak plank sat a gorgeously charred chateaubriand steak, ringed with a Della Robbia wreath of assorted fresh vegetables and a fluted border of mashed potatoes, browned under the salamander flame. For other special occasions we went to Luchow's off Union Square in Manhattan, where our menu was always herring or pea soup, sauerbraten or schnitzel, strudel or the apple pancakes dramatically prepared at the table, a performance I still recall in the sharpest detail.

There were more ordinary, local places we went to just for convenience, like kosher-style delis for salami or tongue and eggs, franks and beans and sandwiches of rolled beef, pastrami or corned beef. And there were also the Chinese restaurants even then mysteriously popular in Jewish neighborhoods. It annoyed me that my parents always chose only among the same dishes: egg roll, roast pork, egg drop or wonton soup, chicken, shrimp or subgum chow mein, moo goo gai pan, lobster cantonese, fried rice and ice cream. Curious about the other dozen or so offerings, I insisted on trying something new each time, thus discovering how much I hated the gravy-laden egg foo yong and slippery chop suey, but loved soft, juicy chunks of beef with crunchy green peppers.

Later, as a food writer, I tried to find explanations for the Jewish love of Chinese food, coming up with a combination of reasons that had to do with the appeal of family-style eating and sharing, low prices and, most of all, I think, the familiar flavors of Canton's softly cooked onions and celery, chicken and rice, and kreplach-like wontons in chicken soup, to say nothing of tea. Then, too, there is an absence of dairy products in Chinese cooking. Even though no Jews going to such restaurants could be kosher, they probably had not developed a childhood taste for dairy products alongside meat. I have heard conjectures that Jews in New York learned to love Chinese food because of the proximity of the Lower East Side and Chinatown, but how then to explain that same predilection among Jews in France, Denmark, England and Israel? Or could it simply be true that one of the Lost Tribes of Israel settled in China centuries ago?

Given the amount of food talk, it might be hard to believe that it was rarely our main topic of discussion, but more or less side commentary layered into talk of the personal and public issues of the days between the Great Depression and World War II: sympathies for union organizers and contempt for the company goons who beat them up and why one should never cross a picket line which, to this day, I cannot bring myself to do; the scandalous behavior of our next-door neighbor's daughter who joined the Communist party; the importance of collecting tinfoil from cigarette packages and chewing gum wrappers to be made into bullets for the Spanish Loyalists; and of Adolf Hitler's hysterical outcries that crackled and faded, screeched and swelled via shortwave radio, rendering what little German my parents might grasp totally unintelligible, but leaving no doubt about the chilling portents.

On the personal side were arguments on the endless rifts between my father and my mother's family, about which she was excessively sensitive to the point of tears, or a temporary financial bind, or why Fred Allen was funnier than Jack Benny. In my senior year at Midwood High School, there was bitter wrangling about my being allowed to go to college out of town because I was a girl, one more reason for me to be resentful and infuriated by gender inequality. Little did my father know that what he most feared might happen away from home took place in his own living room directly under the bedroom in which he was asleep. It was a lesson I kept in mind when raising my own child, realizing how little parents can know about what is really going on.

What I also kept in mind was the danger of assigning a role to a child so early in life that he or she acts to make good on the prophecy. In my case, I felt compelled to be the "Daddy's girl" everyone said I was, often leading to the guilt of mixed loyalties during parental arguments, and, ultimately, I now believe, in my mother and I being pitted as adversaries, however subtly. That I rarely opened up to or sided with her kept me from ever asking about her hopes and happinesses, her dreams and frustrations as a dedicated wife, mother and homemaker who in today's world surely would have been a canny entrepreneur.

Despite all of the emphasis on food, it never occurred to me that it would become my career, mainly because I never knew such a career existed. I was aware that someone produced recipes for newspapers, but I did not equate that with writing, which was one of the two pursuits I considered, although I had no idea what I wanted to write about. My other choice was doing research in either genetics or microbiology. I was and remain intrigued by what can be seen when one knows how to look, especially the idea of magnified, microscopic life and the chromosomes that practically seal our fates.

Often as a food critic, I was accused of being clinical in my approach, my idea being to spread everything out, eye (or taste) it coldly and see just what was real or fake, good or bad. That is why I often ordered every dish on a restaurant menu in the course of many visits, or one day collected 104 corned beef and pastrami sandwiches in New York to see which deli had the best meat and sandwich-building technique, and then described and evaluated each in details that admittedly might seem clinical—as compared to romantic or poetic—for better or for worse.

A Taste of New York

"**R**EMEMBER, BABY! The name of the game is beat the house!"

It is a midwinter afternoon in 1945 and I am at Tondelayo's, a sleazy supper club on New York's West Side, the neighborhood of jazz boîtes, watching the rehearsal of the club's new act. The starring chanteuse is Tondelayo Levy, a slim, dusky and sensuous mulatto who is married to the club's owner and who can probably do just about anything better than she can sing, judging by her nightly performances with a five-piece combo as guests dine on typical nightclub food—awful and overpriced. I am with Irving

Hochberg, the comely, stocky, zoot-suited Big Man on Campus who was my fiancé during this, my sophomore year at New York University, and one of the few men around, the army having rejected him as 4-F for an unapparent physical impairment.

A senior at the same school, Irv, a brilliant, funny and canny tummler, is testing careers as a gag writer, a magazine publisher, a gambler or a garment manufacturer. It is the first pursuit that led him to create the routine of jokes and lyrics for Tondelayo and to be partially paid in due bills, credits for meals we would consume on dates. Ordering the most expensive foods such as steak and lobster that gave the management the smallest profit margin—thus beating the house—was Irv's partial revenge. Never was I to order chicken or fish (cheap food in those days) or begin with soup instead of shrimp cocktail. Just as at any eat-all-you-want buffet, we never wasted space on our plates with potatoes, rice, macaroni, coleslaw or baked beans.

Beating the house was a principle Irv followed in other areas: he taught me to sneak into movie theaters by telling the ticket-taker that I had lost a hat during a previous showing, then going in to "search" and getting lost in the dark, a trick easily accomplished in those days of continuous performances. Never mind he had very well-to-do parents in Yonkers who gave him his own car and that he earned enough cash from extracurricular efforts to take me to the Astor Roof when Harry James played, or to the Café Rouge of the Hotel Pennsylvania to hear Tommy Dorsey, or to the Glen Island Casino if I spent the weekend in Yonkers. He also was able to afford a five-dollar-a-week furnished room off Washington Square where we whiled away spare hours and occasionally squeezed in some schoolwork. When I proudly reported his successful ploys to my mother (skipping the rented room), she was furious and declared Irv a Communist and an unfit beau.

With us at Tondelayo's is Irv's cousin Irving Grossberg, the composer and performer of the music for the act, who is just beginning to morph into Larry Rivers, actually his third name, as he had been born Yitroch Loiza Grossberg. Dark haired, gaunt and often in a marijuana haze, he wields a saxophone far more deftly than a paintbrush and sports a tiny, slim beard that runs from his lower lip to the tip of his chin and for which he has two explanations: it cushions his lip and chin when he plays the sax and, also, women find it titillating when he performs oral sex. If he has any ambitions to paint, I've never heard about them. Hanging out and double-dating with him and Gus (Augusta), his pregnant wife-to-be, we always call him Larry, taking sides against his parents, who protested the name change by ignoring it.

The change annoyed them especially at the couple's spring wedding, a madly packed affair of effusive, first-generation Bronx Jews in a kosher Romanian restaurant on the Lower East Side, with music supplied by Larry's reefer-stoked band and deep, meaningful soul kisses for all the women from the groom himself. These were bravely delivered between aromatic courses of *icra de sucra* (whitefish roe caviar), jellied calf's feet, matzoh ball soup, garlicky beef *karnetzlach*, thick belts of skirt steak and a choice of vegetables that included stuffed *derma*, kasha varnishkes and four kinds of potatoes: mashed with fried onions and schmaltz, latkes, french fries or fried silver dollar rounds. In my memory, it was the sort of event Fellini might use as a model if he ever applied his talents to Jewish weddings. Perhaps not even Fellini would have guessed that years later, Berdie, Gus's chubby dumpling of a Jewish mother, would replace her daughter as head of Larry's household in Southampton and be celebrated naked, sagging flesh and all, in several of his paintings.

Of all of the strategies that have influenced my menu choices through the years, Irv's was certainly the most improbable and bizarre, as was that entire heady, hectic year from the autumn of 1944 through the summer of 1945. Throughout, I dashed all over the city wearing a Sloppy Joe sweater, pleated skirt, bobby socks and saddle shoes tied with plaid shoelaces with bells on them. Yet I drew on the experiences of that year repeatedly in negotiating my way through New York's publishing, entertainment and restaurant worlds. It was a year that shattered naïve illusions and imparted just the right amount of skepticism necessary to a journalist. Not that I guessed it would prove so significant when I was living it. Writing a memoir is like Monday morning quarterbacking. It is much easier to trace past events that determined present circumstances than to predict which current activities will inform our future.

My personal coming of age, fraught with the tensions of school, anxiety about a career, love, sex, perfidy and the lure of the City, was played out against the larger drama of world events and undoubtedly was tinged by the prevailing public spirit of feverish anxiety and alternating moods of victory and despair. In many ways to Americans at home, being at war took on some aspects of a nervous holiday as during a blizzard or a blackout when all bets are off and real life will count again only when the disaster has passed. If it was a decisive, action-packed year for me, it was a far greater one for world history, what with the death of Franklin Delano Roosevelt (April 12, 1945), the only president I clearly remembered; V-E Day, marking the defeat of Germany (May 5), the sickening accounts and photographs of Nazi concentration camp horrors; our atomic bombings of Hiroshima and Nagasaki; and finally, on August 14, V-J Day, with the surrender of Japan, when I joined the hysterical swirl of humanity that jammed Times Square.

Had it not been for my running around the city with Irv, being constantly shocked yet amused by his exploits and ever the loyal moll, I sincerely believe my college education would have been a waste. Not being allowed to go away to school and undecided about a career and, most of all, wanting to get to Manhattan,

I enrolled in what was then the N.Y.U. School of Commerce, Accounts and Finances on Washington Square. This forerunner of the now highly regarded Stern School of Business taught in my day what I regarded as crap courses, at least for undergraduates—copywriting, typography, layout, production, media, marketing and the attendant research methods—supplemented by liberal arts "survey" courses, deemed important because "even in business" one must be able to talk about art and literature. Who knows? Even a latter-day Babbitt might have heard of Rembrandt or Shakespeare.

The mistake in choosing this curriculum was entirely mine, the only parental guidance having come from my father. He decided I should be an advertising copywriter because I wanted to write and also because his own business put him in touch with a successful copywriter at the Milton Biow Agency. Four things about her convinced my father it was the job for me: she was a woman; she had a private office with a secretary; she earned $125 a week; and, the clincher, she was Jewish, as was the owner of the agency, a double rarity in those days in that field. He arranged an interview during which she gave me a pep talk, and, beguiled by her dark green walls and mahogany credenza, I figured, why not? My only addition to the scenario was that I might like to write for a newspaper or a magazine and so majored in marketing and minored in journalism, not realizing how much more valuable a broad liberal arts curriculum would have been. But I was pleased that my degree would be a bachelor of science that seemed weightier than mere "arts." Despite what it says on my diploma, however, my real major was New York City.

The Commerce schedule left me plenty of free time to explore the streets, alleys, shops, art movie houses, cafés and restaurants of Greenwich Village, during which I developed an affection for the area I would choose to live in for the next fifty-nine years, and still counting. Most teachers were professionals, working for agencies, publishers and the like and so classes ended at one o'clock. There were some liberal arts electives that could be taken in late afternoon or evening, thereby providing excuses for me to put off my daily return to Brooklyn. I and a few friends always took one late course so that we could have dinner in the Village and explore such bygone restaurants as the original Sea Fare on Eighth Street, where black waitresses wore colorful bandanas on their heads and the dessert of the era was a rum-flavored chiffon pie called Nesselrode. In the intimate downstairs setting of Mother Bertolotti's on West Fourth Street, I ordered a different dish each time, sounding confident even when I had no idea what to expect. Thus I became the object of great laughter when Bel Paese arrived as a small triangle of foil-wrapped cheese, an unthinkable dessert compared to the spumoni and tortoni my friends had. Of course I knew what it would be, I lied, downing it on saltines with feigned gusto.

Also, before meeting Irv, the school schedule enabled me to hold part-time jobs selling cosmetics at the Abraham & Straus department store in Brooklyn and, through N.Y.U., being hired to take surveys for several market research firms. Having successfully phonied a percentage of the questionnaires by answering them myself, I also might interview a girlfriend, asking, "You're a forty-three-year-old man who makes fifteen thousand dollars a year. What do you think of New Jersey blueberries?" The most difficult were media studies for Daniel Starch. I had to carry around about twenty magazines and go through Grand Central Station looking for the right mix of respondents (age, sex, level of dress, occupation) and ask if they had seen and remembered this or that advertisement, many of which were control dummies that had never actually run. Small wonder that I still have a healthy suspicion about reported results of such research.

Irv's schedule in accounting classes also allowed time to operate primarily as the business manager or publisher of the university's humor magazine, *Varieties*, a *New Yorker* knockoff that ceased publication in 1950 and that contained many cartoons, satires, campus gossip and an occasional short story, all done by students in the various colleges. It was a much-coveted job that he inherited from two friends who had held it before they graduated; one, Martin Ragaway, was already a well-paid screenwriter in Hollywood. It was coveted because there was income attached in the form of kickbacks from the printer and the agency that placed advertising in college publications, all said to be shared with the professor who was the magazine's faculty adviser. Part of Irv's job was to see that advertisers got the position they requested and also that none would be offended by editorial matter. When I later worked at *Seventeen* I was less shocked by blasts and demands from advertisers than were my fellow, still idealistic junior editors.

In addition, Irv produced a paperback collection of *Varieties* cartoons that he sold through distributors and peddled in person to newsstands from bundles stored in the trunk of his car. My role was to help and though I was not officially on the staff, I fitted copy, proofread and regularly went with Irv to the printer on East 45th Street, then known as Printers' Row. There we worked late until the magazine was put to bed, after which we went across the street for steak at Pen & Pencil, the hangout of working newsmen.

It was at *Varieties* that Irv's gag-writing efforts flowered, for although not the editor, he supplied cartoon captions. These efforts were far more serious when his contacts enabled him to get into the rehearsal studios of such famous radio comics as Milton Berle, Henny Youngman, Morey "Yucka-Puck" Amsterdam and several lesser lights. We would ride the upper deck of the Fifth Avenue bus from Washington Square to NBC and CBS studio rehearsals, where Irv would accost some lackey if not the comic himself and reel off the jokes he had created. What amazed me first was the ease of access in New York if one had moxie and knew the right people, and, even more astonishing, that no one evaluating a joke ever laughs. The listener would look serious and weigh the idea with a poker face, much as a garment manufacturer fingers the goods to judge quality. Accepted jokes earned five or ten dollars in cash and, as far as I knew, none was used without payment although no agreement appeared in writing.

Occasionally Irv would get an assignment to write a routine for a special show, and I was able to contribute to one that ran on Washington's Birthday. Comic: "They say George Washington was the father of his country. I thought that was Errol Flynn." Considering that I have met young people who never heard of that dashing film star, it seems best to point out that at the time, he was the object of several paternity lawsuits. When I told my mother that a joke of mine would be on the air, she scolded, "We pay for you to learn, not to write jokes!"

By then I was incurable. Always fascinated by what made something funny, a holdover from the serious respect my father had for comedians and the value he placed on a sense of humor, I still regard stand-up comics as the world's most skillful psychologists, able to know exactly what words will open the synapses of a given audience and evoke the involuntary reflex that is a laugh. I loved the technique of formula routines such as mother-in-law and wife jokes, and openers like "My room was so small that . . ." and "A funny thing happened to me on my way to the studio . . ." Now I use some of those devices to work humor into my public speaking.

In between jokes, there was gambling, another of Irv's pursuits that led me to strange places, none more so than the second basement of a luncheonette near school (now the site of N.Y.U.'s Bobst

Library), where there was a floating crap game that sometimes spilled out into the park. The game stopped in that location after a cop walked through this illegal activity, scooped up and pocketed the cash on the ground, then went off without saying a word.

Big-time gambling involved basketball, laying bets and odds, giving and taking markers, knowing if players had agreed to shave points and, for good measure, scalping tickets to games at the old Madison Square Garden on West 50th Street near Eighth Avenue. Because of that speculation, Irv had been barred from the Garden the previous year by its thorny president, Ned Irish. But as Irv did not exactly look like Public Enemy Number One, and there were crowds at the many entrances, we always got in, I to be left high in the rafters as he went down to hedge his bets. After games, we went around the corner to the Hotel Belvedere, as the lobby was the meeting place for payoffs between bookies and their clientele. Of all his nefarious endeavors, Irv's betting against our school was the one that shocked me most, as I still had enough rah-rah-rah spirit in me to consider it treachery. As he predicted, I got over it.

If there was nothing bigger to gamble on, Irv made his own game. Sitting in the school lounge, Lassman Hall, he might say to some nearby friend or stranger, "I have a fin that says you don't know the meaning of mellifluous." Or, "For a sawbuck . . . Will the next guy coming into the room put his left or right foot over the threshold first?"

Testing his father's occupation as a garment manufacturer, Irv, whenever he could get some cotton fabric, had it made into something like shorts or blouses that he sold to apparel chains, all much in need of merchandise during wartime shortages. If that took up the least time, it proved his most prophetic venture, as the garment industry is indeed where he realized his desire to get rich.

My biggest problem was that I was painfully shy and quiet with

Irv and his friends, all fast-talkers with their own special lingo and to whom topping each other was a game. As Irv frequently said in a sly, aspirated Charlie-Chan-Chinese dialect as bragging got under way, "Ah so, Eugene Fliedman, Number One fliend of my childhood. You speak first, you lose! Velly stupid!" Before such evenings, he pleaded with me, "For God's sake, baby, talk, will ya? None of the guys think you can." Several times on dates one or another of those guys would become a contestant on a radio quiz show through a producer who was a friend. They were always given the answers, thereby winning enough money to take six or eight of us to dinner at the Lobster, Oyster and Chop House, Ruby Foo's or Phil Gluckstern's around Times Square. No wonder that when the $64,000 Question quiz show scandal and Charles Van Doren's ethical lapses stunned the public, my reaction was, "What else is new?"

What I somehow neglected to tell Irv during our early dating and engagement was that I was still writing to two old flames in the service, including romantically lean and lanky William Schlifman, for whom I had carried a torch since I was sixteen, mostly because he treated me miserably. The other was a dashing meteorologist in the air force on whom I had a crush because he treated me wonderfully. It seemed cruel to drop any of our men in service, even though they were at U.S. bases, and irrelevant to upset Irv about something so inconsequential, since both were remote.

His biggest mistake was deciding to spend his last free summer after his graduation as a camp counselor, a job he loved. I would not join him there, having avoided the whole regimented, athletic notion of camp throughout my childhood, and so I took surveys and went to summer school. He came to New York on days off, for which he reserved a room at the Hotel Dixie in Times Square (now the Carter Hotel) because it was known as a shack-up joint, which, he said, sounded functional. I would tell my parents that I was visiting my girlfriend in Rutherford, New Jersey, and was never caught, a miracle because my uncle Henry was the Dixie's house detective.

But between Irv's visits, the prodigal William returned from the air force and announced that he loved me and wanted to get married. On Irv's next day off I told him that I was seeing Bill. It was a hot, airless August night (before air-conditioning), and our room was even more stifling because of the cloying sweet scent of Yankee Clover, a popular cologne that I had doused all over myself. Neon lights from 42nd Street below flashing against the ceiling lent the final touch of seaminess to this endless, sweaty night as I withstood Irv's incredulity, anguish, reproaches and exasperation with what I guess seemed my rather casual approach to the subject. As he prepared to return to camp the next morning, we said good-bye through tears on a platform in Grand Central Station and I feared he might commit suicide by jumping in front of an oncoming train. But as my great friend Irene Kamp, the editor at *Seventeen*, said when I told her about this long after, "They never do . . ."

Two weeks after V-J Day, when I was nineteen, Bill and I eloped to Greenwich, Connecticut, where eighteen was the legal age of consent rather than twenty-one as in New York, and we were married in court by Judge Oswald P. Gunnarson, Sr. Neither of us wanted a wedding of which his family would surely disapprove. ("We did not move to Riverside Drive to have our son marry a girl from Brooklyn," his mother told mine the first and only time they spoke.) Also, with my obsession about being my own boss, I wanted to do something legally binding that my parents could not undo. Or even if they could, would not, but I could and did ten years later.

I feel redeemed to say that Irv survived to become wealthy, happily married and the father of several children, although he died much too early in his energetic, productive life. Every five or seven years, he and I had lunch and he always asked if I ever regretted my choice. I could honestly answer never, because I think I felt a certain alarm about marrying him, sensing that he would support me admirably and house me in Westchester, where I would become a housewife through my own inertia and DNA. Fortunately, by marrying Bill, who became a student on the G.I. Bill of Rights, I had to work, a lucky necessity indeed.

Nibbling Around the Edges

HAVING TRIUMPHANTLY CAUGHT the man I had been crazy about since I was sixteen, I was as optimistic about the future as the rest of the peace-enthused world. At roughly 6 feet 4 inches, William Schlifman had long wanted to change his name to Shelby, which he thought sounded classy, although he never acted anything but Jewish until years after our divorce, when he became not only an Episcopalian but also a minister. What drove him to the name change right after our marriage was his parents' abysmal treatment of me and my family, and he felt the change would hurt them, as it did. I disliked Shelby, so we

opted for Sheraton, unwittingly presaging my future career in
home furnishings. My big regret is not having resumed my maiden
name, Solomon, when we divorced.

He was lean and languid and had the high-cheekboned good
looks reminiscent of Errol Flynn or John Lindsey. Women rarely
could resist his considerable charms and not many tried, even some
of my best friends, and men instinctively distrusted him. As I was
to discover, he never met a woman he could say no to and, in fact,
sex proved to be his long suit, leading me to decide that he probably
was a sexual idiot savant. He proved neither to be good at, nor
interested in, much else, being the sort of dreamer who went from
one job and career to another, for which he blamed my refusal to
give up my career and move to a little house in the suburbs to work
as a housewife and mother. As much as I intermittently wanted to
save the marriage—making up was fun—I intuitively resisted his
plan for our life, knowing I was young enough to wait for children
and feeling insecure about our future.

Like many such marriages, when it was good it was very, very
good and Greenwich Village proved the perfect backdrop. After marrying, I no longer wanted my parents to support me, although they
did pay the tuition for my last two years of college, which I finished
in night classes. I found a job as a copywriter for an advertising
agency specializing in retail ads, my assigned groups being jewelry
and furniture stores around the country. The main problem was finding an apartment in the Village, close to New York University, an
area I already loved. But as in any part of New York, empty apartments were almost nonexistent, there having been no new construction during the war. Finally, after days of walking the scorching
late-summer streets, we snared a one-room basement apartment that
was furnished, a somewhat exaggerated term for the chipped, broken
and sawdust-trailing pieces that filled the room and enabled the landlord to raise the controlled rent to sixty-five dollars a month. With

windows fronting on the street, we were often awakened on Saturday nights by drunken tourists rapping on the glass and when coal was delivered, dust and even lumps fell into the room, especially if we forgot to close the windows, which, though barred, permitted one slender burglar to enter and take a Rolleiflex camera and a radio.

That all of this was considered romantic was due to the popularity of the 1942 film *My Sister Eileen* (later the basis of the Broadway musical *Wonderful Town*), based on the partially autobiographical short stories by Ruth McKinney about two career-girl sisters from Ohio who lived in a Village flat similar to ours. Only my mother was upset by that choice, regarding the Village as an area of questionable types that included, in her words, mixed marriages, fairies (then the kindest designation for homosexuals), artists and, her personal hobgoblins, Communists. Her assessment sounded promising to me, and my father seemed unperturbed, commenting only, "So you want to be a bohemian!" I have lived there ever since, more bourgeois than bohemian, establishing a career, divorcing, remarrying, raising a son and progressing from tenant to landlord and from a wide-eyed newcomer to a misty-eyed old-timer.

Approaching my sixtieth anniversary as a resident, I regard my first decade in Greenwich Village as a Golden Age and perhaps the last of the area's celebrated creative heydays. Peace had settled in, the Depression was over, servicemen returned home and the whole world was as optimistic as I was. Despite its gently quiet, laid-back atmosphere, the pleasantly shabby Village simmered with creative foment. Abstract Expressionist painters congregated at the Cedars (formally the Cedar Street Bar) and psychoanalysts abounded, as did crafts such as weaving on huge looms that left little space for living, and throwing and firing pottery in one of the innumerable classes and clubs, home kilns having been forbidden as fire hazards by most landlords.

The Village offered us easy fun, what with inexpensive but col-

orful restaurants, cafés, bars and nightclubs, art movie theaters that
served free coffee from silver urns, and a vast temptation of shops
offering books (new and used), handicrafts, antiques and pastry.
Panhandling drunks were more amusing than threatening, especially at the San Remo, our hangout bar on the corner of Macdou-
gal and Bleecker Streets, where would-be poets like Jay Spenser
cadged drinks and stole sandwiches from patrons as he beguiled
them with poems about girls with "pink legs and pale minds."

The books we argued and discussed ad exhaustion until four
o'clock in the morning ranged from Philip Wylie's *Generation of
Vipers* (1942) with its vitriolic swipes against American icons like
mother and the common man ("the hero's backside") to Norman
Mailer's *The Naked and the Dead* in 1948.

Completely free were the alfresco attractions of Washington
Square Park, where on weekends we read the Sunday *New York
Times*, sketched, listened to poetry readings, folk guitarists and
political diatribes, and collected money for the 1948 presidential
campaign of Henry A. Wallace. We watched in awe as Eleanor
Roosevelt left her apartment on the park's west side to walk the
presidential black Scottie, Fala. Those of us with a taste for poetry
cherished glimpses of e. e. cummings's shiny bald head as he
emerged from his home in tiny Patchin Place, and of the bumbly,
good-natured W. H. Auden, who lived on Cornelia Street. It was
heady stuff indeed for a nineteen-year-old Brooklyn transplant and
almost good enough to make me forget that where I really wanted
to be was Paris.

The biggest drawbacks about our apartment besides space and
privacy was the DC electrical current that made it difficult to find
appliances like broilers, mixers and toasters that would work, and
the size of the so-called kitchen. Always interested in cooking and
expecting to be good at it, and with a husband who loved to eat, I
looked forward to creating epic meals, if only on weekends. Week-

day nights we rarely ate at home, what with my night classes, but relied on food counters in drugstores such as the Bigelow Pharmacy, where great London broil was the Thursday specialty, Chock full o' Nuts near N.Y.U., the Waldorf Cafeteria on what was then Sixth Avenue and, across the street, the all-night Jefferson Diner. What passed for a kitchen in our apartment was enclosed in a closet so small that it held only a small sink with a drainboard overlapping one of the three burners on a small, low horizontal stove that had an oven hardly big enough to hold a sixteen-pound turkey. When the oven door was open, there was no space to stand in the kitchen. One had to stand in the living room and bend around to baste or turn. A tray-size shelf on the inside of the door provided the only work space, and so I opened the gate-leg dining table where I could chop, arrange and roll out pie dough. A refrigerator and dish cupboard shared space with a clothes closet and chest of drawers in a dressing room. Later, when I began to write about the wisdom of having a well-equipped kitchen, I always feel a bit guilty or embarrassed, knowing great kitchens do not great meals make.

Undaunted, I began my life as a cook, planning ambitious meals drawn from my mother's repertory and from *The Settlement Cookbook*, the only cookbook she gave me, a Jewish-American compendium by Mrs. Simon Kander. I also found inspiration in *Gourmet*, a relatively new magazine that I found on a local newsstand and that instantly intrigued me into trying to prepare dishes I had never tasted. With articles by M. F. K. Fisher, Lucius Beebe, the Maine poet Robert P. Tristram Coffin, Leslie Charteris, creator of The Saint, and Rex Stout of Nero Wolfe fame, I developed a new food sensibility. Many years later when I started to write about travel, I gained similar insights from Lesley Blanch and William Sansom—not learning how to write from them but, rather, learning how to perceive.

Making one of the true amateurish mistakes, I once tackled a chicken curry recipe from *Gourmet* that called for powdered coriander. Not having the slightest idea what that was, I stopped cooking midstream and ran around to all of the foodstores in the area, including the food section in John Wanamaker's, the department store then on Broadway and Eighth Street, all to no avail. I finished the curry without missing whatever flavor coriander would have imparted, having learned a lesson about checking all necessary ingredients before starting to cook. Had I known then what I know now, I would have bought a bottle of readily available mixed pickling spices and extricated the gray round coriander seeds. But now, of course, I can get coriander almost anywhere.

After two months in our apartment, we invited my mother, father and brother for Thanksgiving, my first big effort for guests. The turkey proved to be the first problem. It was too big to wash in the kitchen sink, so I used the bathtub, lifting the bird out and not realizing it was full of water that cascaded down all over me. Then there was the problem of fitting it into the oven, a trick accomplished when I cut off the rear end so the door would close. I prepared chopped chicken livers as an appetizer; cream of shrimp soup based on a frozen Campbell's product to which I added fresh shrimp, cream, butter and sherry; candied sweet potatoes; creamed white onions; stuffing and string beans, all of which was cooked in shifts and kept warm by being piled pot-over-pot on my two usable burners. Dessert was taken care of by my mother, who brought her celebrated lemon meringue pie. I am not sure that anything I ever accomplished afterward made my parents so proud of me as they were that day.

Although my forty-dollars-a-week salary was considered good for someone my age, and Bill had a stipend from the G.I. Bill as long as he attended Long Island University, Friday was my payday and we always ran out of cash on Thursday. Our strategy was to return all the deposit bottles we had saved that week and buy something inexpensive like eggs or a can of Broadcast Brand Corned Beef Hash to eat that night. Rationing remained in place for a short time after the war, and I learned to use coupons wisely for ingredients such as meat (but not chicken), sugar, flour and butter, for which margarine was sometimes a substitute. In those days, by law, it had to be sold uncolored. The ghostly white fat came with a packet of powdered coloring that one could blend into the softened margarine. Later it was packed in a plastic sleeve that included a capsule of liquid color that could be burst and squeezed through the mass, a most un-*Gourmet*-like cooking step.

When we felt flush, we tried some of the fancier Village restaurants, including Charles's on Sixth Avenue just about where the Jefferson Market is now, the Brevoort on the corner of 8th Street and Fifth Avenue, the Amen Corner of the Fifth Avenue Hotel, now 24 Fifth Avenue, for an elegant eat-all-you-want Sunday brunch and, in warm weather, the wide, flower-trimmed sidewalk café, Le Jardin du Perroquet, in that same hotel. For casual meals we went to the Helen Lane Tearoom on the site of what became later the Coach House and is now Babbo. When someone had a car we might have a special occasion meal at the Claremont Inn on upper Riverside Drive, but there, as at many of these pricey outposts, we generally ordered the cheapest things on the menu— usually chopped steak or seafood crepes—and wondered what all the fuss was about. There was a lesson in this, namely not to go to such places until one can afford to try the things they are best known for. Another splurge was to take the subway up to the old Tip-Toe Inn on Upper Broadway and buy turkey sandwiches on rye with coleslaw and Russian dressing, then eat them in a taxi going back to the Village. Often, in our unabiding longing to visit France, we went to the little bistros on Ninth Avenue and in the

50s—Paris-Brest, Brittany, Le Berry, Rey & Pierre and Bonat's near the main post office—to choose from the offerings on hors d'oeuvres wagons and pastry carts, to the recorded songs of Piaf and Trenet.

Tired of writing for the advertising agency and identified as a home furnishings writer, I was hired for that work by *Good Housekeeping,* in the department known as the Decorating Studio, where it didn't take long for me to discover I was in over my head. The editor, Helen Sells, was a colleague of and successor to the well-known decorator Dorothy Draper, and the offices were done up with her trademarks—dark green walls with plaster white trim or rooms wallpapered with cabbage roses. Sells was a serious decorator and like most others in the department had been trained in art and design schools. Modern design and architecture were just beginning to emerge after the war, with the classic modern furniture designs of T. H. Robsjohn-Gibbings, Charles and Ray Eames, Eero Saarinen and Ed Wormley. The modern houses I had to describe in copy, all elegantly photographed by Hans Namuth or Suter of Hedrich-Blessing, were usually in California or around Chicago in suburbs such as Evanston, Glencoe and Highland Park. It was not the sort of home furnishings copy one does for small stores in assorted Podunks, and Sells, who was almost always drunk on the gin and vodka she kept in medicine bottles, was so furious about my writing that it took ten years for me to get over being afraid to put down a single word. One memorable exchange occurred when she briefed me on the salient points of a house, pointing out a big window wall in the dining room. I described the room as having big windows, causing her to scream, "My dear! We simply do not say big windows!"

"What do we say?" I asked, near tears.

"Wide fenestration" was the answer.

Sells was almost mortally terrified of the magazine's legendary editor, Herbert Mayes, who always seemed sardonically jovial to me. But she trembled and took an extra swig from her medicine bottle when one afternoon he ordered her to have his office walls painted *and dry* by eight o'clock the next morning. I could almost see myself there all night, fanning those walls.

Nevertheless, it was that job that got me into the magazine world and so was even more pivotal in my life than my marriage. In addition, I discovered that I loved interior decorating when I helped round up accessories and worked on photography shoots. I decided I would like to be the editor, not merely the copywriter, and so I enrolled in a one-year night course at the New York School of Interior Decorating, now the New York School of Interior Design. I loved everything about it, including classes on architecture and furniture history and periods, the intricacies of textile weaves, wallpapers and carpets and the correct terminology and quality points for various types, arranging rooms and drawing to scale for floor plans and, most of all, mixing colors to match various samples and learning about hue, tone, value and shades. I still enjoy working with color and drive painters crazy in my house, even though most of the walls are white. There are whites and then there are whites, and if a painter doesn't listen to me, I fool around with his paint cans after he has left for the day, adding a bit of burnt umber here and a drop of chrome yellow or Prussian blue there, then reporting to him what he must do in the morning.

I was reminded of my color mixing experiences many years later when I was working on *The German Cookbook* and trying to perfect a recipe for the Bavarian midnight snack, goulash soup. It needed more caraway accent but the mix was already so dense with flavor I would have had to add a ridiculously large amount of seeds to have an effect. What the soup needed was opening up, lightening in a sense, so another flavor could show through. I remembered techniques of color mixing, when the addition of a little white or light gray can allow room for another shade to register. I suddenly thought of vinegar, of which two tablespoons did the trick, separating flavors and making room for caraway.

Having earned a certificate as a decorator, I was hired as the home furnishings editor at *Seventeen,* a most fortuitous place to be just then. Still run by its founding editor, Helen Valentine, who sold her idea to Walter Annenberg, *Seventeen* blazed trails not only in teen fashions but in graphics. Following such illustrious art directors as Jan Balet and Ralph Daddio, Cipe Pineles bought art from a group very different from those used by other slick magazines, especially for story illustrations, and she won countless art directors' awards for work by Ben Shahn and David Stone Martin as well as for her innovative layouts. Being around the art department, I discovered the fun of collecting beautiful objects, as humble as a found stone or bent branch, or as costly as a Baccarat paperweight. I have never stopped collecting stuff, with a strong preference for what Ludwig Bemelmans once called "beautiful dreck."

Two later editors—Alice Thompson and then Irene Kamp, who became the best woman friend I have ever had—were the first to make me feel good at my job. They sent me to Chicago and Grand Rapids furniture markets twice a year and occasionally encouraged me to report on aspects of home furnishings far too advanced for our teen audience—primarily for my own interest and career. Although home furnishings that interested teenagers were generally restricted to re-dos of their own rooms, the bigger field, incredibly enough, related to hope chests. As hard as that is to imagine today, teenage girls collected silver flatware and to a somewhat lesser degree china, glass, bed and bath linens and blankets without any particular mate in mind, and stored much of it in Lane cedar chests, one of the magazine's most loyal advertisers. Silver and hope chests were my provinces, which meant I regularly visited silversmiths, china and glass factories and linen mills to see new designs. I was also mastering the ropes of press parties, switching from Canadian Club to Scotch as Beryl Walter, the food editor and my mentor at the magazine, had advised me to do, along with when to arrive and how long to stay. At several events I was introduced to James Beard, then struggling to earn a living as the colorful, operatic chef-spokesman for Presto cookware, among other products.

In my spare time, I messed around in the magazine's test kitchen that adjoined an office I shared with Beryl. When she left, the editors asked if I wouldn't like to do food as well as home furnishings, since I seemed so interested. Of course, I said yes, but not before insisting on making a trip that Bill and I had saved for during two years of frugality—three months for our first look at Europe. I was so determined to go that I was prepared to quit. Alice Thompson not only agreed but offered to give me half pay if I would visit the European china, glass and silver firms that were our advertisers. That enabled us to buy lots of Hans Wegner furniture in Denmark, an enormous service of Arzberg china in Frankfurt, and who can remember how many blankets, lamps, accessories and other tchotchkes, plus handbags, gloves, scarves and everything else that was so cheap for Americans in those days.

The plan we followed was to fly to England for two weeks and pick up a small car—a Hillman Minx—that we would drive in Europe and then send home. We planned to return on the *Queen Mary* so that all of our purchases could come back with us. From Harwich, we took an overnight ferry to Esbjerg in Denmark, drove across Jutland and Fyn and ended in Copenhagen. Then we continued to

Germany and on to Switzerland, Italy, Spain and France, ending up with two weeks in Paris before going back to Southampton for the voyage home.

That some of our most interesting visits were those made to the companies I wrote about convinced me forever that one gets more out of a trip by pursuing work than merely pleasure, primarily because one gets to know new people on the common ground of an interest rather than as strangers. I still cannot understand why vacationing lawyers, doctors, teachers, gardeners or whatever do not try to meet at least a few of their counterparts when abroad.

And of course, there was the food with revelations that have lasted a lifetime. I expected to have great meals in France and Italy, but had few ideas of what I would find elsewhere. The first surprise was the delicate, clean-tasting fare of Denmark, something I knew in New York only from smorgasbord tables at then-popular places such as Copenhagen, Castleholm and Gripsholm, among a few others. I was beguiled by the fresh-air flavors of dill and caraway and the exquisitely fresh seafood simply prepared. That meant not only the famous tiny shrimp, *rejer,* but the sautéed speckled sole that is *rödspaette,* and the poached codfish served with horseradish and melted butter. Among the meats, I was stunned by corned, poached duckling topped with frozen whipped horseradish cream, a sort of sherbet that sizzled down over the hot duck meat, and I could not get enough of *fransk boeuf,* a thick filet mignon topped with almost invisible slices of rindless lemon and a stick of butter verdant with chopped parsley, a sublime blend of flavors as one cuts through the butter and lemon to the beefy juices.

I also was invited to a dinner that has perhaps done more than any other to make me think about meals and the way they are served. It was in the home of Piet Hein, a well-known poet, scientist and artist whose cartoons lampooned the Nazis during their occupation of Denmark and who also designed and decorated porcelain, among many other talents. He had a lovely home in the Copenhagen suburb of Hellerup, a Scarsdale-like place of gracefully large villas and amazing gardens, which had, like so many in northern climes, flowers of the most intense colors. Our invitation came via a mutual friend, Just Lunning, who ran Georg Jensen's in New York and turned it into the unofficial Danish consulate. He was also at the dinner, which was served only by candlelight as is the Scandinavian custom. It was a huge room with a soaring skylight. The table was teak and the only linen, other than napkins, was a vermilion, hand-embroidered center runner on which were flowers and candles. The meal began with the tiny shrimp just then in season, with about one hundred piled onto two slices of crisp-crusted French bread thickly spread with sweet Danish butter. There was lemon and some dill for those who wanted it, but since none did, neither did I, anxious, perhaps, not to mask the shrimps' sweet essence. The main course consisted of boiled new red potatoes, each of which had had a thin band peeled off around the center; all were strewn with dill and held in a big pink terra-cotta bowl then fashionable and known as a Portuguese batter bowl. Along with the potatoes came creamed wild mushrooms—whether morels or chanterelles, I can't remember—gathered by the family just that day. That was, most deliciously, it, and a revelation about appreciation and simple perfection that I never forgot. Assorted Danish cheeses were pre-desserts, served with celery, radishes and cucumber and grapes as the only fruit, and then *kransekage*, baked almond-paste sticks zigzagged with white threads of sugar icing. Throughout the meal we drank cleanly astringent aquavit washed down with sun-gold Carlsberg beer.

There were other mind-changing meals on that trip, most of them as simple as a slice of pâté de campagne, the little rolls of creamy cheese, Petit Suisse, and good French bread that we bought for picnic lunches along the drive. Later trips to France saw that general availability decline as mass production took over. As Yves

Saint Laurent said many years ago when I interviewed him on the
subject, "Today you need an address." You did not need an address
to find the best food in 1953.

Among other meals in France that I remember most fondly was
perhaps the simplest I ever had—one perfect whole black truffle
sous les cendres, roasted under ashes, and served in a flower-folded
linen napkin as a very costly main course at Rotisserie La Perigour-
dine on Place St-Michel in Paris. I also recall with much longing
the first two bistros I visited in that graceful city: Restaurant des
Beaux-Arts and Restaurant des Sts-Pères. At the first, I quickly
joined the regulars who paid for a napkin once a week, each to be
held in a separate small marked drawer, and where I ate memorable
boeuf bourguignon and navarin of lamb. Years later, reading A. J.
Liebling's Paris memoir, *Between Meals,* I was pleased that he also
favored that restaurant, crediting it as the place where he learned
how to eat well on a tight budget. I'm sure he would be as upset as
I was to know that it is now an antiques shop.

For sheer charm, the winner was Restaurant des Sts-Pères on
rue des Sts-Pères and Boulevard St-Germain with its zinc bar
mounted over a colorful inlaid marble base, its tile floor and
incomparable artichokes vinaigrette, *cervelles au beurre noir* and a
gratin of veal with cream and tomatoes. When homesick for that
personal icon (now a Sonia Rykiel shop), I turn to the evocative
photograph of it taken by Paul Child, husband of Julia, for
Waverly Root's seminal *The Food of France.*

Another lesson in simplicity came in a raucous workers' bistro
in Limoges, where we were guests of Harold Haviland, whose
porcelain factory we visited. What I couldn't resist were *radis au
beurre* as I watched workers eat them, picking up a speck of sweet
butter on knives, then drawing them through one radish at time,
leaving the butter behind and dipping all into *gros sel.* It was to
Harold Haviland that we also owed our stupendous meal at the

only three-star restaurant we sprang for on that trip—Restaurant La Pyramide, also known as Chez Point, in Vienne. Hearing that we were driving about four hours out of our way just for that dinner, Harold Haviland phoned Monsieur Point, to whom he supplied china, and the meal he laid out for us is as fresh in my mind as the flavors were on my palate that evening. We began with the maestro's famed parade of four appetizers, starting with a meaty pâté en croute and then foie gras in golden brioche, the first time I ever had that unctuously fat and supple liver. Then came feuilleté niçoise, layerings of flaky puff pastry with a piquant filling of olives, tomatoes and anchovies, and finally garlic- and parsley-scented escargots. Another first for me were the delicate, cloudlike dumplings, quenelles made with pike (*brochet*) in a rosy crayfish-accented sauce Nantua. Point's version of quenelles became the benchmark for me. Fortunately, I found some equal to his at La Grenouille in New York and in Léon de Lyon in Lyon. By the time we finished roasted quail, cheeses, frozen desserts and pastry, we were happy to have reservations at a local hotel, being as drunk on food as on wine. Alas, the ghost of those dishes, and of Point himself, who died two years later in 1955, haunted me when I returned in 1978 to review Pyramide for the *Times* and found that everything about it had declined even though it retained its Michelin three stars.

As memorable as the trip was, it spelled the real ending of my marriage. With all due respect to Yogi Berra, romances and marriages are usually over long before they are over. We fought, vowed to break up, "but not yet," almost daily, with the biggest argument occurring in Hamburg over what I recognized as one of the best breakfasts of my life, not withstanding the tears. Never had I had more amazing ham and eggs than those prepared in that marvelous port city's railroad station, done pancake style with ham and eggs fried together, all golden edged with crispness. I operated on two levels, holding my part in the argument but keeping eye and palate on the eggs. I have since returned to Hamburg twice, although not in many years, and each time had breakfast in that station, never to be disappointed by the *Spiegeleier mit Schinken*.

Which is more than I can say for the man. About four months after our return, we separated for the third and final time. A year later I went to Mexico for a divorce and following the convictions of a truly liberated woman, I divided everything we owned in half. My only regret was that when I gave him the top half of the double boiler, I also threw in the lid.

A Table Before Me

DURING THE EARLY MONTHS following my separation from Bill, I was depressed by the thought of how much time I had wasted—ten years that could have been full of more exploration and productive fun. Still, I realized that it was the marriage that had enabled me to get out of Brooklyn and into my own New York apartment and to develop a career. I moped around the offices of *Seventeen* for a few weeks until editor Renie Kamp advised, "Nothing has to be a mistake. It's what you do with what you've done that counts."

Certainly I had a lot to be happy about. I had our twelfth-floor apartment on Washington Square Park. Facing south, it overlooked a

skyline of water towers populated, I fantasized, by mischievous water
sprites. Air-conditioning was still a rarity, so on hot summer nights, I
opened the bedroom window and caught elusive strains of jazz ema-
nating from Eddie Condon's club on West 3rd Street, which I overlooked, distance lending enchantment to wails of brass and reeds.

To further cheer myself up, I planned a return trip to Paris,
traveling alone just to prove to myself that I could.

Most of all, my work at *Seventeen* gave me solace and a sense of
accomplishment, especially when I was appointed the food editor in
addition to handling the home furnishings department. All too soon,
however, that unbridled pleasure was marred by the arrival of Enid
A. Haupt, sister of the magazine's owner, Walter Annenberg. Impec-
cably dressed, usually by Dior, an orchidist whose hobby was performed by her gardener and an important collector of Impressionist
paintings, she apparently had decided that she needed a real purpose
in life and that it might as well be as publisher of *Seventeen*. She
seemed gracious if slightly patronizing, and we were more amused
than annoyed when she had a fitting for custom-made shoes during
an editorial meeting and made statements such as "No matter what
happens to *Seventeen*, I'll always eat," to which I could only reply,
"Me, too."

Although Enid Haupt began making Renie's life miserable early
on by usurping editorial functions, I had no trouble at the start and,
in fact, had a few entertaining meetings with her and her husband,
the Wall Street financier Ira Haupt. Savvy about art and other cultural pursuits, he appeared a diamond in the rough—stocky, dark
and with macho good looks. Learning that all three of us would be
in Paris at the same time, Enid Haupt asked me for a favor: Would I
keep her husband company for lunch at Relais des Porquerolles to
have that Michelin two-star restaurant's famous bouillabaisse? He
hated to miss that on any visit to Paris and she was sickened by the
sight of that massive seafood preparation. Feeling like a gastro-

nomic hetaera, I was picked up the next day in a limousine that stretched beyond the front of the little Hôtel du Quai Voltaire, where I was staying.

Porquerolles in my memory was a shimmer of majolica colors— purple, green and yellow—with tropical fish tanks here and there. Haupt had ordered the bouillabaisse in advance and it was served traditionally in two courses. We began with the soup ladled from a tureen and redolent of wine, saffron, garlic, fennel, accented by the warm, heady aroma of the sea. Croutons and a bright garlic, oil and cayenne-spiked rouille completed the course before the masterpiece arrived. It was presented on a huge, thick cork plank with a well shaved into the center to catch the juices of the pink and silver whole fish, the stone gray mollusks and roseate crustaceans. Authentically enough, there were no shrimp or scallops, and Ira Haupt assured me that it had been made with the spiny scorpion fish, rascasse, which is a key ingredient to aficionados. (Some purists also claim no shellfish belongs in bouillabaisse but I hold with those who exclude only shrimp and scallops.) The meal was a savory, slurpy orgy during which we talked about baseball, art, food and more food. Years later I was saddened to read that the chef-proprietor, Alain Zick, committed suicide in 1966 because Michelin had downgraded his rating. It was in the tradition of other overwrought French chefs who were embarrassed by their failures, most notably the seventeenth-century cuisinier, François Vatel, who took his own life when a fish did not arrive in time for the lunch of Louis XIV, and more recently in 2003, Bernard Loiseau of the Burgundian restaurant La Côte d'Or, who did the same because he received a Michelin downgrade.

Soon after my return, Enid Haupt fired Renie, took over the editor's function herself and announced to me that she was going to do a food story; she was so intent on keeping the subject a secret she would not divulge it even to me. I was insulted and quit immediately. I realized that I had spent far too much time writing for teenagers when an adult audience would enable me to treat food and home furnishings more fully. Leaving taught me a valuable lesson: to keep a job and do it well only as long as it worked for me, because jobs belong to management and are only on loan to employees. The idea of lifelong loyalty to a company seemed out of date even in 1954. I never again became sentimental about a company I worked for, no matter how much I enjoyed being there.

Before long I was hired as the managing editor of a supplement division of *House Beautiful* that each year published four bridal magazines and two each on gardening and architecture. Half of the artwork came from back issues of *House Beautiful* but was used in different contexts, and we produced the rest as writers and editors. After the sixth time I had to write the correct order for a wedding receiving line, I had had enough and began a twenty-year stretch as a freelancer. Fortunately at the same time, I also had begun reviewing restaurants for the weekly magazine *Cue*, writing under the name of Martha Martin because the editor, Jack Keating, thought Mimi Sheraton sounded improbable. As I look back at some of my earliest and most amateurish columns, it was just as well that Martha Martin took the blame during the first eighteen months before I reverted to my own name.

About a year after my divorce, my personal life improved considerably, with a blossoming love interest in the form of one Richard Falcone, a merchandise manager at Gimbel's, whom I had met at several trade shows while I was still married and working at *Seventeen*. Among the many departments he handled—major appliances, radios and televisions, toys, sporting goods and fashion fabrics—were several with merchandise I covered: unpainted furniture much used in teenagers' rooms and linens and tableware that was collected for hope chests. When it was necessary to borrow these pieces to photograph, Dick and I met for a cup of tea or lunch and developed well-disciplined crushes on each other that remained unacknowledged until after my separation.

An Italian-American born in the Bronx, Dick's first language was Italian and he spoke it fluently, which I found exciting when we ate at the old Rocco's in Greenwich Village and at Romeo Salta's, to me the best Italian restaurant New York ever has had. Dick taught me the subtleties of dining as Italians do—no pasta "on the side," no soup and pasta in the same meal, which contorni (side dish vegetables) go with which main courses, never to put cheese on a seafood sauce, and so on, customs well known now, but not in those less sophisticated times. Exciting, too, were his strong, compact good looks that suggested the smooth intactness I admired in Italian men. Considered a most eligible bachelor at thirty-six, Dick exuded a certain rakish, insinuating freshness typical of many Bronx men, a trait that I found titillating. Even my mother fell for him at first sight, despite her barely muttered, knee-jerk disapproval of my dating someone who was not Jewish, a position from which she rapidly retreated; my father didn't care about such things at all. A wonderful date, Dick introduced me to many operas, and by way of contrast, to the people-watching delights of the old Sherry-Netherland Hotel bar, the hangout for floozyish kept women who were stashed in apartments along the anonymous length of West 58th Street between Fifth and Seventh Avenues. That a few knew him and came over to chat added spice.

As we got to know each other better (something Dick said occurs only when a barrel of salt has been shared), I became aware of the irony that while I was running around New York peddling jokes between 1944 and 1945, Dick was landing on Normandy's Gold Beach and later spent forty-five frozen days in a foxhole during the Battle of the Bulge. Months later, as a radio operator in an armored vehicle, he was in one of the first reconnaissance units to cross the Remagen Bridge. Between Remagen and a return to New

York and Gimbel's, chance circumstance took Dick to Paris, where he was discharged and offered a job at the U.S. Information and Education Office, the organization that planned and advised on cultural and educational matters for returning G.I.s. He spent a year in Paris, witnessing the gradual recovery of postwar France, and his work gave him the chance to spend time with Gertrude Stein when she volunteered to host G.I.s.

Among our many compatibilities was our shared love of food. We liked almost all of the same things, except that I hated tripe, which I thought tasted like bad breath, and he hated noodle kugel, which he dismissed as sweet pasta. Although I was used to the generous portions of food my mother served, I was surprised by Dick's idea of suitable quantities, which became obvious the first time I went to his mother's apartment for dinner. Seated at the table with Dick and his older brother, Tom, I was served a huge, delectable bowl of zucchini that had been simmered with a little olive oil, then stirred in with beaten eggs and Parmesan cheese as a first course. I asked for a spoon to serve Dick and Tom. Just then Irma Falcone emerged from the kitchen with two equally large bowls for her sons. "That is your portion," she said. She never ate vegetables, so I asked how much zucchini she had bought for three of us. "Five pounds" was the answer.

That I had no trouble finishing it before going on to a baked pasta and one of her specialties, veal cutlets Milanese with crunchy potato croquettes, convinced Dick that our relationship was worth pursuing. Years later as my mother-in-law Irma sent me the recipe for those cutlets, explaining that grated Parmesan, salt and pepper are mixed into the breadcrumbs, and that the breaded cutlets are then pressed between two plates and chilled in the refrigerator for two or three hours before being fried in Mazola corn oil and served with lemon wedges.

If Dick needed further proof of my credentials as a trencherperson, he got them on two other occasions. Once when we were back at my apartment after an opera and hungry, I prepared eggs and he asked how many I had scrambled for him. When I answered four, he asked with a big satisfied smile, "How did you know to do that?" But it was at a dinner at Enrico & Paglieri, a spacious, beautiful restaurant that was on West 11th Street, that he proposed. Our dinner began with some prosciutto and ripe honeydew melon, then went on to full portions of linguine with white clam sauce and continued with Florentine-style steaks and cool green beans glossed with oil and wine vinegar. "You're okay," he said as I finished everything. "Wanna get married?"

By that time we had rented a summer house in Wainscott on eastern Long Island and, just in case, we obtained a marriage license. The weekend before it was to expire, we called Renie and Louis Kamp, who were in nearby Hampton Bays, and invited them to be witnesses in the living room of Elmer J. Butcher, a justice of the peace in Sag Harbor. Then we called our parents, and I announced to mine, "Guess who eloped again!"

As my marriage to Dick and my career as a food critic for *Cue* and the *Village Voice* and later as a consultant both to the Four Seasons restaurant and to New York University Hospital advanced, so did my hips and waistline. Writing about food gave me just the excuse I needed to eat. It was, after all, my job. As a fat kid who slimmed down in high school in time for dating, I had my ups and downs on the scale and lived through many diets, the first of which was in a thin paperback irresistibly titled *Eat and Grow Slim*. It advocated a well-balanced 1,100- to 1,400-calorie-a-day regime that I followed assiduously, becoming as thin as I would ever be (about 120 pounds) until I began to eat in the Village, after marrying Bill. Intermittently, I tried other fashionable diets. I ate nine oranges (sixty-three a week) and one buttered baked potato a day, and as I peeled my way through the menu, my office began to smell like an orange juice factory and my fingernails took on a gilded hue. Another diet required bunless hamburger for breakfast, one cup of cottage cheese for lunch and, for dinner, six prunes. There were weeks of just hard-boiled eggs and grapefruit, another that allowed all meat but nothing else and another suggesting everything but meat.

Sometimes I subsisted only on bananas or ice cream, and once prepared a drink said to approximate mother's milk. Before there were diets named Atkins, Pritikin, Ornish and South Beach, there were DuBarry, Rockefeller, Mayo, Duke and, later, Stillman, Solomon and Scarsdale. I found Metrecal quite satisfying when whipped with ice cream in a blender as Slim-Fast is now and both proved good accompaniments to club sandwiches. The only diet I didn't try was one that fashion photographer Paul Weller claimed models swore by: swallowing wet, wadded cotton balls with huge amounts of water that caused the cotton to swell, thereby leaving the stomach full—a trick pre-dating the cellulose "graham" crackers that I also tested. Throughout, I searched for clothes that were flattering or, finally, for some that just fit, and I suffered the humiliation of skinny friends who ate with me and declared themselves full after six asparagus and a green salad. "I feel so fat . . . Thank God I don't have to eat dinner tonight," or "I'll have to go on a diet after this," were the sort of remarks they made, never realizing they might hurt someone so overweight. It was somewhat as if they had complained about a bad pedicure to a friend who was missing both legs.

Thinking back, I must admit to having subliminally felt a sense of power that went along with being heavy, as though the more mass I had, the more space I occupied and so controlled. There were even certain questionable but definite benefits, as when trying to make way through a crowd. My ability to do so without consciously trying and with no elbowing or other physical contact became apparent when I instinctively walked interference through an aggressive crush of a crowd pushing its way into the premiere of *Apocalypse Now* at the 1979 Cannes Film Festival with Dick and our son, Marc. I automatically moved slowly but surely as the crowd parted, and Dick and Marc followed in my wake, an eerie phenomenon causing Dick to suggest that I might have a great career as a linebacker. I also told myself that if I ever lost weight, I would emerge smoothly preserved in fat, the central thin core of me being a kind of confit.

I have lost sixty pounds since leaving the *New York Times* some twenty years ago, when I topped the scales at 205. It took three years to lose forty-five pounds with a low-calorie balanced diet interrupted only when I intermittently reviewed restaurants for *Condé Nast Traveler,* and I have kept them off. What finally prompted me to lose weight was a view of myself in a hairdresser's full-length mirror when I was seated and wearing one of the salon's floral print robes and realized that I looked like a slipcovered club chair.

I was determined to follow no formal diet but resolved to make the lowest possible calorie choices (low in both carbs and fats), day by day, meal by meal, minute by minute, and just to move downward on the scales without a specific goal. Upon seeing the thinner me, several magazine editors asked me to write about my experience, but all backed out when they heard it had taken three years. "Couldn't you get it down to three weeks?" was the gist of their suggestions, with one friend saying, "Are you kidding? I have to do it in three days!" Apparently moderation is not dramatic enough advice to sell magazines or books.

Not only has the weight stayed off for ten years, but I recently lost an additional fifteen pounds in five months with the help of Dr. Atkins's low-carb diet, so far my favorite of all regimes. I am sure that one has to be moderately sensible in following his plan, but I am also sure that at least some of the current nay-saying is the hype of advocates of other merchandisable diets or spokesmen for purveyors of pasta, bread, potatoes and sugar, all greatly curtailed on the Atkins plan.

As much as I minded being fat as an adult, being fat as a child was much worse and undoubtedly was what led to shyness and my hating to dance or play sports. Perhaps all of us who were over-weight as children consider ourselves fat for the rest of our lives, no matter how slim we become, partly because we still feel our once expansive girth, as people are said to feel sensations in a limb long after it has been amputated.

Whenever my varied freelance assignments and Dick's heavy schedule at Gimbel's permitted, he and I traveled, with Italy always the high spot, especially when we visited his mother's family in the Abruzzi town of Vasto, high on a cliff hanging over the Adriatic Sea, and Troia in Apulia, where his father, Francesco Falcone, was born. Dick's Abruzzese cousin, a horticulturist, invited us to a dinner for which his wife prepared tortellini in brodo, the meat-filled dumplings adrift in a fragrant chicken broth and sprinkled with grated Parmesan and parsley. We felt downright spooked to find it tasted exactly like his mother's soup back in the Bronx, something I think of when purists say Italian dishes here can't possibly taste like those in Italy because of different qualities of ingredients and, of course, the air and water. Recalling the flavors of her childhood, my mother-in-law apparently adjusted seasonings until she arrived at the taste of home.

We were less fortunate in Troia, where we were invited to lunch by a woman who had been a nursemaid-caretaker to Dick's uncle, who had died a year before our visit. She lived in a home that con-sisted of a bedroom and a kitchen–living room. Meals for guests were served in the bedroom, where a big table covered with a white appliquéd cloth was drawn up to the bed on which Dick and I were seated while his two cousins sat on chairs. We began with the deli-cious Pugliese pasta classic, orecchiette tossed with bits of broccoli di rape, olive oil and garlic. What followed was perhaps the worst thing I have ever had to pretend to like: cold, white land eels, thin, hard and with fuzzy fins along the edges and doused with a watery tomato broth. They reminded me of stiff, hairy fingers that had committed some bloody mayhem before being chopped off a hand. No sooner did I dutifully polish off one portion than another was heaped onto my plate. Only accompanying mouthfuls of good coarse bread enabled me to push the whole thing down.

For our first Thanksgiving together in 1955 we went to Havana, where we took in gambling casinos and the sex exhibitions then de rigueur, especially one that starred the renowned superman who became the subject of a story I wrote for *Avant-Garde* under the pseudonym Francesca Milano. We had both been to Cuba before we met, and shared a love of the music and the languid, sensuous tone of the beautiful Old Havana downtown, with its pastel patinaed buildings and its rainbows of stained glass fanlights. We also relaxed in the tropical lushness of shuttered rooms in the Hotel Nacional, where we sipped mellow *añejo* rum as though it were Cognac. Our lunches beside the pool of that grand hotel consisted of cold, black-tipped Moro crab claws dipped into homemade mayonnaise and a shared coconut shell filled with vanilla ice cream, shaved coconut and a slathering of hot fudge sauce. For dinners we shunned pretentious continental restaurants and went to the famed grocery store-café, La Bodegita del Medio, a seedy spot where generations of visitors had tacked souvenirs onto the wall, mine being a ribboned lock of hair hung there on a previous visit. There, and at small family restaurants in the countryside, we feasted on pit-roasted pig, chicken fried with garlic, thin, crisp and salty fried plantains, black beans and rice and lime-accented avocado in salads with tomatoes and jalapeño peppers, finishing with a cooling dessert of guava shells and cream cheese.

As we knew that my apartment building (which Dick had moved into) would soon be torn down, and felt that we were about to get serious and have a child, we moved to a huge floor-through apartment in a brownstone on West 12th Street, just a few doors away from what later became the James Beard House, Jim by then being a friend. Like so many food writers living in the Village at that time—John Clancy, Craig Claiborne, Sally Darr and the great *New Yorker* food reporter, Sheila Hibben—we often met at the original Balducci's on Greenwich Avenue near the Avenue of the Americas, peering into one another's shopping carts and trying to guess what would be cooking and for whom.

Always thinking up travel boondoggles and inspired by the earlier publication of the Pan-American Airways *Complete Round the World Cookbook* by Myra Waldo, I got the idea for the *World-Wide Restaurant Cookbook*, which just might make it possible for me to eat in every restaurant in the world. SAS agreed to provide me with first-class tickets, and no sooner was the first leg of my journey planned than I discovered that I was pregnant, fate being generously cruel enough to grant me two mutually exclusive wishes. Although SAS said they would wait for me to do the book after the baby was born, I declined, feeling I wanted no such obligation hanging over me at that important time. I gave the project to Charlotte Adams, a friend and much respected food writer, and her dedication in the book reads, "To Marc Christopher Falcone, whose arrival on this earth gave me a chance to go around it."

Because the reviewing schedule at *Cue* would have meant too many evenings away from our son, and missing his feedings, baths and bedtime reading, I gave up the *Cue* assignment in favor of an easier one at the *Village Voice*. In addition, I also had a one-year assignment from Georg Jensen to develop a bridal registry service in the store, and at the same time I became a research consultant to the Four Seasons restaurant as it was being planned, forming a connection with Restaurant Associates that went on for several years and included research for the Tower Suite, the hot-dog chain Zum Zum, which I named, and Trattoria.

When Marc was fifteen months old, SAS executives, knowing

how much I had wanted to do the restaurant cookbook, made me an offer I thought I would have to refuse. They asked me to write an overall guidebook based on a series of city portrait pamphlets to be distributed to passengers. The pamphlets included only the basic minimum suggestions on history, customs, sights, hotels, restaurants, shops, nightlife and museums, and they felt I would have to go to any of the cities I did not already know to enlarge the scope of the book. That I was able to accept could have been credited to the right confluence of the stars in the guise of my stellar support team: Dick, who enjoyed my career as much as I did his; our blessed housekeeper-nursemaid, Maria Dawkins; our sage pediatrician, Dr. Sidney Q. Cohlan and my generous parents, who all came together to take good care of Marc.

The day I went to the SAS offices to plan my itinerary I felt like a kid turned loose in a candy store. Nothing lifted my spirits more than a ticket to someplace, leaving being as exhilarating a thought as arriving. Skipping most of Europe because I had been to all cities necessary for the book except Vienna, I chose to roam mostly through the then Soviet Union, Asia and the Middle East. That resulted in the longest airline ticket I ever saw, with booklet after booklet stapled together for a three-and-a-half-month itinerary routed as follows: New York, Copenhagen, Moscow, Copenhagen, Tokyo, Hong Kong, Bangkok, Phnom Penh, Singapore, Djakarta, Calcutta, New Delhi, Bombay, Karachi, Cairo, Beirut, Istanbul, Vienna, Copenhagen, New York. And then there were the side trips: Kiev, St. Petersburg when it was still Leningrad, Kyoto, Hakkone, Kamakura, Osaka, Nagoya, Siem Reap, Surabaya, Bali, Benares, Agra, Jaipur, Elephanta, Alexandria, Luxor, Aswan, Baalbek and Damascus. Were it not for the resultant book, *City Portraits: A Guide to 60 of the World's Great Cities*, I might wonder if I hadn't dreamed that trip.

From a career standpoint, it surely was the most exciting,

instructive and defining event in the twenty years I freelanced between my work at *Seventeen* and my joining the *New York Times* in 1975. Nevertheless I was at first apprehensive about doing it alone and also feared I would miss Dick and Marc so much that I would quit partway through. Although SAS had offered Dick a ticket for the entire trip or to join me wherever he could, his work at Gimbel's and the thought that at least one of us should be around to share responsibility with my parents made his acceptance impossible.

My apprehension was short-lived, however, as I realized that there would be SAS personnel in many cities to make arrangements and perhaps accompany me on some forays, as well as contacts made through friends in many cities. In addition, of course, there were telephones that enabled me to call home every few days. Inevitably there were times when I was really alone, but I came to enjoy that as I would in later travels. To travel with someone you love and are completely compatible with is an incomparable joy and celebration, but being alone offers certain compensations. Not the least is being able to do exactly what you want to do without considering anyone else. More important is that when alone, I seem to form clearer and more lasting impressions of the new sights and customs I observe because I am more open and have not talked them out, explained them and put them away in a familiar context.

One of the main problems of traveling alone relates to my specialty—eating in restaurants. When I had to do this on my own, I called or had desk clerks call and explain that I was a woman alone who had always wanted to dine in that restaurant and asked if I could have a table. Never did it fail to get me a reservation, I and was afforded the most considerate service and attention.

SAS also offered to send home my purchases city by city so that I could shop with impunity, never worrying about baggage. When I once phoned Dick, he reminded me that I had already sent home sixty-three boxes of one sort or another, and I was not too sur-prised, since boxes seemed the most useful form in which to collect examples of a craft. You can always put something in a box, even if it is another box.

The only catch to the SAS offer was that I would have to pay all expenses other than airfare, which meant a costly tab for hotels, meals and other incidentals, including transportation other than by SAS or Thai Airways, then a subsidiary. To cover expenses, I con-vinced Joe Baum at Restaurant Associates to hire me to do a com-plete report on all of the foods and foodways I came across, including collecting menus and buying cookbooks, food magazines and any reasonable amount of specialized utensils. Although my fee would amply cover my expenses, I obtained two other assign-ments: to write articles on four cities for *Mademoiselle* and to buy samples of folk art for Just Lunning, who wanted to establish a folk art department at Georg Jensen. Thus was I able to spend time with artisans such as batik fabric printers in Bali, painters of traditional wooden tropical fish, the extraordinary lacquerware producer Yamada Heiando in Tokyo, brass workers in India and women who produced embroidery at home in Kiev.

In early August 1960, I began my odyssey. After spending a few days in Copenhagen to make final arrangements with SAS, I was off for two weeks in the Soviet Union, then at its most secretive and anti-American, as Gary Powers's U-2 spy plane recently had been shot down and was on display in Red Square.

In those days, all travel arrangements within the Soviet Union had to be made through Intourist, the government agency in charge of travelers, and one paid in advance to buy coupons cover-ing all expenses, including hotels, restaurants, guides, transporta-tion and cars. The only exceptions were a few semi-private restaurants not included in the Intourist package where one paid cash. I was fortunately placed in the famous old National Hotel close to Red Square, and on my first afternoon, before meeting anyone from the SAS office, I walked out, guidebook in hand, to find the GUM department store and a recommended restaurant. I was stunned to discover that I could not decipher any street signs, this being my first experience with an alphabet I could not read. The guidebook, written by NBC reporter and Moscow correspondent Irving R. Levine, included a chart of the Cyrillic alphabet and I went back to my room and memorized it, working out key words that would remind me how each Cyrillic letter sounded. By way of example, PECTOPAH, pronounced "restoran," clued me that P was R, C was S and H was N. Once I developed a few more such key words, I was able to find my way around.

Other than being bitten by bedbugs at my Leningrad hotel and being told that there was no Russian word for such insects when I complained at the desk, I had no mishaps and found the people in markets and shops, streets and parks, delighted to see Americans, despite the official stance. They reminded me of southern Italians in many ways, earthy and of peasant stock and eternally downtrodden by whoever was in power, church, state, feudal lords or modern bureaucrats. Food was scarce and the only place for quality products was the Central Market in Moscow, where farmers who had fulfilled their government quotas could sell their surplus at uncontrolled prices, for which they saved their best mushrooms and eggs, fruit and peppers. Restaurant service was dreadful. I often sat for thirty minutes before an order was taken, only to be told in another half hour that whatever I had ordered was no longer available. Except for delicious breakfasts of cheeses and salamis, smoked and salted fish, eggs and vegetable salads with sour cream, I took to subsisting on the plentiful, excellent caviar, great breads, delicious soups such as the variety of borschts and the pungent solyankas (meat and pickle soup-stews) and the excellent Georgian black tea and ice cream. The only really good restaurants in Moscow were non-Intourist establishments such as Arrarat, which served Armenian food, and Aragvi, the first place I tasted Georgian food with its contrasts of walnuts and coriander, garlic and chilies, yogurt and dill. Its flatbread was baked against the walls of an igloo-shaped stone oven that was the forerunner of the tandoor, which the Central Asian hordes brought with them as they swept down to India.

To go to Tokyo, I returned to Copenhagen for a flight over the North Pole to Japan, a twenty-six-hour route pioneered by SAS in those days of four-engine planes. Anyone who says that travel holds no surprises because of the speed of airplanes (as opposed to trains, steamships and, I suppose, horse and carriage) has to match me a marvel of a journey that began in Denmark, ended in Japan and had an unexpected two-day stop at the North Pole. When two engines went out, the pilot announced that we would be landing at an American air base in Thule, Greenland, which, as he was only the first of many to remind us, was just ten miles north of the magnetic North Pole.

We landed at the U.S. air base in charge of the Ballistic Missile Early Warning System—the enormous BMEWS radars. The permanently frozen ground—permafrost—looked like packed mud and as it was September, it was the season of perpetual twilight— no sun, no darkness. We were lodged in very comfortable barracks reserved for VIP visitors such as entertainers and congressmen and were issued parkas because we were all dressed for the hot and humid early autumn in Japan. Hosted in groups by air force officers, we ate in their club, which had excellent hamburgers, and were taken to visit some of the twelve Danish families who lived there, representing their government, which owned Greenland, and who served us open-face sandwiches and tea. The biggest thrill was going into the BMEWS offices, carved out of ice under the polar cap, a luminescent and soaring cave-shaped place.

A few of us were grouped with two particular officers as guides, one a captain and helicopter pilot who had heard that I had something to do with food. As the conversation progressed he made an offer: if the next day I would prepare marinara sauce and pasta from ingredients in their storeroom, he would fly me over the polar cap in a helicopter, although, he warned me, I would have to sign a release. Alas, the replacement plane came from Stockholm all too soon, and I was probably the only passenger to be disappointed at our rescue.

After my arrival in Tokyo, I ate and shopped my way through Japan, marveling at the exquisite arrangements of food and the crunchiness of the two methods of frying—tempura done in a batter, and katsu done with a breading of dried, coarse breadcrumbs, panko. Of all the kaiseki—tea ceremony dishes—I had, the one that was the most beautiful was a big wild matsutaka mushroom, grilled and nestled in a bed of long pine needles and topped with a meringue snow peak, to me almost as impressive as the elegant rock gardens, torii gates, Buddhist shrines and Ise temples.

While traveling by car from Tokyo to Hakkone, I tried to instruct the driver to stop in Yokohama at the Sex Drugstore, a shop recommended to me for the purchase of French ticklers for several friends who had requested them. Since Ichiro, my driver, saved face by falsely claiming to speak English, explaining what I wanted without resorting to the most vulgar hand language was almost impossible, and only a G.I. passing in the street who had learned some Japanese explained it all to him. The adventure in the Sex Drugstore, with other American tourists asking me what gadgets served what purposes, became a story in *Eros* upon my return.

In Hong Kong all of the great things I had heard about its cuisine were true, but there were titillations by way of braised bear paws, beggar's chicken cooked in mud, feathers and all, and a roasted pig feast at which I committed the gaffe of starting to eat the meat. I was told that only the crackling skin was for the patrons—the meaty carcass belonged to the help and was sold to the poor, who purchased it at the kitchen door.

In Thailand I began a practice that proved fascinating and educational on several other stops. I hired or was invited by cooking teachers to take part in classes, private or public. I began in the big country kitchen of Terb Xoomsai, a beautiful Thai princess, who cooked for the palace and on television. We spent three mornings together as she taught me to make tiny crackers of pigeon pea flour, the baked palm sugar custard called sankhaya, steamed in a coconut shell, and Thai fruit salad, for which every grape and mandarin orange section had to be peeled of skin or membrane. At first, I didn't like Thai food. Lemongrass tasted like the mosquito repellent citronella, of which in fact it is the main ingredient, cilantro tasted like soap and even the purple basil seemed medicinal. Gradually my palate adapted and I enjoyed the hot green curries and *tom*—soups.

At a Vietnamese restaurant in the Cambodian capital, Phnom Penh, I took another lesson after spending three days viewing all of the temples around Angkor Wat in Siem Reap. The Vietnamese dishes I most wanted to learn to make were ground shrimp and water chestnut balls grilled on sticks of sugarcane, and some of the cool and slippery sweet drinks based on big-eye tapioca.

Singapore was a raffish place indeed, with street food really being sold in the streets and alleys, not as now in food courts. No doubt the new way is more sanitary and healthful, but to sidle up to a picnic table in Satay Alley and have some pork or beef grilled while buying rice steamed in a banana leaf packet and cold beer from wandering vendors had a certain charm I missed on later visits. I also missed the chicken rice stalls along Middle Road, where that cozy comfort food sold for thirty-five cents a bowl.

Sukarno was president of Indonesia in 1960, and Djakarta

looked like a long-abandoned city taken over by squatters. There and later in Bali, there was not a single toilet seat and the only bathing facilities in hotel rooms were big square sort of wells of cold water with dippers. Defying a notice not to take photographs at the Djakarta canal where people bathed, washed clothes and dishes and performed toilet functions side by side, I had to surrender my film to two policemen who generously returned my Leica. In Djakarta, the only noteworthy food was nasi padang—what the Dutch named rijsttafel—at a private club, Wisma Nusantara, where the winning dish was curried ducks' eggs.

In Bali, most food tasted of kerosene, which was just coming into use for small stoves. Except for a meal of roasted pig given by the Tjokorda, or lord, who presided over the artist colony of Ubud, something I had read about in Miguel Covarrubias's book *The Island of Bali*, I lived on freshly made peanut butter, bananas and satays cooked over coals. Much later I tried the durian fruit, a stinking melon that looked like a giant grenade and when ripe smelled like a mix of rotten cheese and overcooked cauliflower. More appealing were various small sweet candies, somewhat like gumdrops, formed into beautiful little ornaments as offering to gods on special altars and the air at all of the ceremonies such as the Monkey Dance and tooth-filings was permeated with the scent of clove-spiked cigarettes.

After the sparseness of Indonesian fare, India was a virtual banquet. Indian food had not yet appeared in much of the United States, although there were some cheap representations in New York. New to me were the spicy tandoori grills, most famously done at Moti Mohal in New Delhi, which was not yet a tourist destination. Served with slivers of fiery green chilies, the meats were moist and succulent against pilaf gilt-specked with saffron. I bought more things in India than in all other countries combined, beguiled as I was by the silks, the papier-mâché of Kashmir and the black-and-silver Bidri ware. I bought the gleaming brass jugs and food carriers that were sold by the pound and old bronze figurines of animals and gods in the Old Delhi market.

In Egypt I immediately fell in love with Cairo, the very different Mediterranean city of Alexandria and the desert wonders and ruins of Luxor and Aswan, so much so that Dick and I have gone back three times. Memorable dishes I tried when I returned home included creamy fattah, baked layers of phyllo, chicken, yogurt and rice, the fava bean breakfast porridge that is *ful mudammas* and the little fried bean croquettes called falafel elsewhere in the Middle East but *tamia* in Egypt. A most special treat was wood-grilled pigeons served in the teeming Khan el-Khalili market and in pavilions along the banks of the Nile.

I had been told that Lebanon had the best food in the Middle East and it took only a few meals to convince me of that. (I awarded a close second place to Turkey.) Whether it had to do with the previous colonial French connection or not, the light oils, fragrant lemons, delicacy of the seasonings and careful handling of food made it seem like a wholly different cuisine from the one represented in New York's Lebanese restaurants. I was privileged to spend three mornings in the kitchen of Georges Reyes, chef at the Bristol Hotel, learning Lebanese specialties rather than the French also on the menu. A city of enormous charm, Beirut offered gorgeous casinos by night and exquisite beaches by day, and it was from there that I went with car and driver across the Bekaa Valley to Damascus, stopping at the Roman temples of Baalbek, where a Druze family shared salted sunflower seeds with me. On our return from Damascus with its stunning Sumerian sculptures and its painted murals of the Dura-Europos Synagogue, the driver and I were starving as we crossed over the border into Lebanon close to midnight. There at a gas station café, we had one of those simple snacks that are so often incomparably delicious—a large, paper-thin round of pita spread with yogurt cheese, or *labneh,* and sprinkled

with olive oil, chopped scallions and mint, then rolled like a long
cigar. That, plus a meal of meze that consisted of forty-two plates,
including boiled sheeps' feet and raw lamb liver, and a dessert of
clove-flavored dates soaked in honey, made Lebanon a high spot
indeed.

I thought it would be funny to spend Thanksgiving in Turkey,
so I did, shunning turkey for the public hammam, or bath, at
Galatasaray with a Finnish woman who worked for SAS. Embarrassed to be the only two women with pubic hair in a land where
that is a mark of uncleanliness, we refused the evil-smelling gray
depilatory offered to us. We stood still, however, for the buckets of
water thrown at our heads preparatory to a scrubbing by muscular
women wearing only towels around their waists who soaped and
pummeled us on a soap-slippery marble platform as we slid into
other patrons. We emerged looking as if we had been boiled and
drove to a spot along the Bosphorus where natives went to taste and
compare various spring waters or sip tea from samovars.

Donner—"ever-turning"—kebob, which the Greeks call gyros,
was then little known in New York, and I was invited to see it being
prepared by an Istanbul restaurant famous for it. At seven in the
morning I climbed down a ladder with a guide-interpreter under
something like a manhole cover in the street and walked along a
winding narrow underground passageway to the butcher's work-
room. There he arranged lamb in three ways—ground, cubed and
sliced into scaloppine, all flavored with onion and salt. On a long
skewer he alternately layered the various cuts of meat so that when
cooked they stuck together and could be cut down the skewer in
long slices. It was succulently delicious as I discovered when I
returned for lunch. My final cooking lesson of the trip was in
the school for Turkish brides run by Ekrem Muhiddin Yegen, the
Escoffier of Turkish cuisine, who had a restaurant below the
school. There I learned to prepare the classic Circassian chicken,

with its sauce of ground walnuts, walnut oil, garlic and a faint blush of paprika and Yegen's celebrated water borek, the thinnest possible boiled phyllo noodles layered with feta, yogurt, dill and butter before being baked.

By the time I got to Vienna, I was so used to the light fare of Asia and the Middle East, which is low animal fats, that I literally ate myself sick at Demels during the pre-Christmas season, when pastry concoctions were at their richest and most opulent.

And then on to Copenhagen for a bite of herring and a shot of aquavit before heading home in new clothes made by a tailor in Hong Kong ("You have very big hips, Missie. Why not admit?") to my young son, who took about three hours to recognize me.

Then it was time to pay the piper by working on the text for the huge travel opus and, in between, finishing my first book, *The Seducer's Cookbook*.

Somewhere in that period, I began to work for the Hallmark Gallery on Fifth Avenue on the site of the present Fendi shop. Belonging to Hallmark Cards, the street level was a retail shop for the company's products and the lower portion was a gallery of the popular arts, a special interest of the company's founder, Joyce Hall. The director, David Strout, a talented painter, photographer and teacher, asked me to help plan the opening show, the Art of the Wedding, because of my bridal magazine experience. He was so inspiring to work for that I freelanced other exhibits based on food (Bread & Wine), design (Design Italian-Style) and crafts (American Needlework, Past and Present), among several others. Again I was traveling, looking for exhibition pieces. I spent a month in Milan with Strout ("I never before had breakfast with someone who was planning lunch and dinner," he told me), talking to architects and designers and gathering material for a story on the city's restaurants for a travel magazine, *Venture*.

It was the Bread & Wine show for Hallmark, as well as research for *The German Cookbook,* that took me to Germany often, never more memorably than one late February when winter stayed late and Easter came early. Munich was a breathtaking sight, as the pussy willows—*kätzchen*—Germans give out on Palm Sunday instead of palm branches were everywhere; spring crocuses blossomed in snowdrifts. Among the welcome sights of this spring season were foods such as green chervil soup on Green or Holy Thursday, chocolate eggs and rabbits decorated with sugar pussy willows and, on Easter Sunday, church altars banked with glass bowls of colored water, each glowingly lit from behind by a tiny candle. I soon realized that most cities have their own seasons and holidays—defining times that make one understand their old architecture and even their food. Following this theory, I did a story for the new magazine *Diversions* called "The Great Indoors," putting myself in the deep freeze for three weeks as I traveled mid-February through the North Sea cities of Amsterdam, Hamburg, Lübeck, Bremen, Oslo, Bergen, Stockholm, Helsinki and Copenhagen. As I arrived at each frozen destination, I was told the next would be even colder and it was, but that chilling weather gave me a new appreciation for schnapps such as vodka, aquavit, genevre and fruit brandies, pea soups and sausages and saunas and snug interiors with rugs and fabrics hung on walls.

While researching *The German Cookbook,* I spent time in the Black Forest near the tiny town of Herrenalb, where a small inn was noted for its blue-cooked trout made with fish caught from a dammed-up stream when they were ordered. Each fish was quickly eviscerated, rubbed with vinegar and poached, turning the skin blue and causing the fish to snap into a ring. While walking through an adjoining town one morning, I was invited to see a minister there who had heard an American was visiting. I agreed, glad to take respite from the piercing cold, only to find the narrow, dark, unheated entrance hall of the house was even colder than the outdoors. As the door opened to the sitting room, there was a bless-edly hot, luminous burst of what seemed to be sunlight but which emanated from the pale yellow walls and light refracted through white organdy curtains. The candy-like, warm scent permeating the room was, as I soon discovered, the combined perfume from vases of freesia and bowls of drying winter apples. The minister's wife served a snack—homemade rosehip wine with a pungent cherry flavor, accompanied by freshly baked big soft and salty pretzels, split and spread with sweet butter. I have been buttering my pretzels ever since.

Usually pleasures define the memories of cities we visit, but trou-ble, if not tragedy, can also give one a lasting link to a foreign place, as I learned when Dick, having left Gimbel's to become president of a ski and tennis company and importer of ski equipment from Ger-many, was on a business trip to Munich. He traveled with members of his company, one of whom called me early one Sunday morning. Immediately I asked, "What happened to Dick?" What had hap-pened was a ruptured appendix. I arranged for my mother and housekeeper to take care of Marc and left for Munich that evening.

When I arrived at the hospital I couldn't believe it was Dick in the bed, looking so wan, sunken, hollow and ancient. He had suf-fered cardiac arrest on the operating table and in the course of the next two weeks would have blood poisoning, pneumonia, kidney failure and, from the blood thinner, nosebleeds so severe his nos-trils had to be packed. I immediately wondered how I would get his body home and how I would tell Marc what had happened to his adoring, beloved father.

Although some day staff at the hospital—the Surgical Clinic of the University of Munich—spoke English, virtually none did so at night, and because Dick had an aversion to German he would not try to speak it. The late British drama critic Kenneth Tynan once wrote that there was an anti-Mediterranean bias implied in all

German cooking but I'd never heard of an Italian who just could not wrap his mouth around a German word. I slept on a cot in Dick's room, and each morning while he was prepared for the day, I walked back to the Bayerischer Hof Hotel to shower, nap, dress, then returned to the hospital, where midmorning weisswurst and afternoon coffee cake were served to patients and their visitors. After three harrowing weeks, Dick, though still weak, was able to make the flight home.

Several years later, Dick, decided to start his own business and reverted to an earlier interest in tableware. He became the exclusive United States importer of Puiforcat silver and Porcelain de Paris china from France, along with crystal from Italy and linens from several sources. We also realized the dream of every true Villager by buying a brownstone with a garden and, for the first time in my life, having a professional kitchen.

Shortly after, I decided to fulfill an ambition to take a course at Le Cordon Bleu, the famed Parisian cooking school. With Marc away at summer camp, I signed up for a six-week course, promising myself about sixty-five meals in Paris restaurants. Classes were held five days a week, and during three, we cooked and ate our results for lunch. It was well-matched group, mostly Americans, although the course was given completely in French. Among us were several cooking school teachers and two young members of the Guste family who owned Antoine's in New Orleans. In addition to enjoying the classes in the rather out-of-order kitchen in which oven thermostats barely worked (the entire school moved and was modernized several years later) we enjoyed going to restaurants together. But for the first week of my stay, I ate every evening with Paula Peck, a friend and the extraordinary baker and cook whose book *The Art of Fine Baking* is still considered a classic. By chance she and her husband, Jim, were also at the Hôtel du Quai Voltaire, and Francophiles that they were, had the most reliable list of good

Paris restaurants that I have ever come across. I recognized being on a roll and joined them in a selection of small, typical bistros, mostly famous—Louis XIV, Au Grand Comptoir, Cartet, Aux Lyonnais, Pierre Traiteur, Allard.

Then I began choosing for the group at the school by sitting on my bed and spreading out before me the Guide Michelin, Waverly Root's *Paris Dining Guide*, the Guide Kleber and Gault-Millau. Kleber was my first choice for ratings, although I checked it against Michelin, then read Root and Gault-Millau for full descriptions. Never have I had a better reputation as a picker. I decided to try restaurants that were considered *cuisines des femmes*, kitchens with women cooks, and listed as such in Guide Kleber and Waverly Root's guide. Said to be the keepers of the flame, they were (and are) lauded as authentic producers of tradi-tional bourgeois dishes, rather than being creative innovators, a province considered more suitable for competitive male chefs. Women were also said to be the producers of the only good beurre blanc, the whipped butter and vinegar froth of a sauce that enhances poached pike or turbot. Years later I returned and did a story about these *femmes* for the *Times* and interviewed Madame Germaine Saunière, at Cochon d'Or, which was near the old Les Halles. Celebrated for her incomparable sole meunière, her roasted kidneys and crunchy, breadcrumb-encrusted pigs' feet, her entrecote and warm cherry and custard clafoutis, she never changed her menu. I asked if she would like to prepare new dishes. "But, Madame!" she said nervously. "I began cooking here in 1929 when I was twenty years old. Three generations have come to me for the taste of my rognons and sole. They would be disappointed if I changed anything."

Of the lessons I learned at the cooking school were three I trea-sure most. The first is that in French cooking one is always balanc-ing flavors, back and forth and up and down so that no one flavor predominates, "Correct, correct . . ." being the admonition old Chef Narses, our teacher, made most often. The second, more minor but aesthetically appealing, is that when making a dish with many different ingredients, such as a stew with vegetables, no two should be cut into the same form, and finally, the best presentations are the simplest, expressed by the chef as he tapped a plate of food he approved of with the accolade *"pas de chi chi."*

Back at home and settled down, I began to write for *New York,* but rarely on restaurants. Mostly I evaluated products, stores and caterers. That research led me to develop what I have come to consider Sheraton's law: Whenever cheating is possible, cheating will occur. The more I delved into how food products were grown, processed or otherwise handled, the more I recognized how one can judge quality by knowing telltale signs. As I interviewed various food purveyors, many of whom had no pretentions at gourmandise and might even be happy at McDonald's, I realized that they could tell more about quality than most food writers who waxed poetic in descriptions. It took a spice dealer to point out the difference between what he called "lousy California bay laurel" and the "true" Turkish bay leaves grown on the sunny side of a hill and from a fresh crop.

George Kinzler, a legendary food buyer at Macy's, and Robert Gumport at Bloomingdale's both said the foods they worried about most for consistent quality were those that came in bulk—caviar, nuts, jelly beans and similar candies, and coffee beans, to name only a few. They worried because with such foods stale can be (and often are) mixed into fresh, or a percentage of an inferior quality can almost invisibly be mixed in with the best. Even now I wonder if a pound of Colombian Supremo coffee beans are all really from Colombia, and all supremo, or if perhaps about an eighth of that pound is made up of inferior

African robustas. It is possible that even a dealer who buys those beans already roasted from a distributor may not know, so difficult is it to tell the difference unless one sees unroasted green beans or is a very experienced taster.

Stories on such topics for *New York* magazine proved to be important stepping-stones in my career, eventually leading to an invitation to join the *New York Times*.

Achieving Critical Mass

My Time at the Times

"WELCOME TO THE ESTABLISHMENT," said A. M. Rosenthal on December 1, 1975, my first morning at the *Times*. As reassuring as such a greeting should have seemed coming from the executive editor, it shocked me: I had always cherished being antiestablishment, whether writing for the early *Village Voice* or Ralph Ginzburg's controversial magazines, *Eros, Moneysworth* and *Avant-Garde,* and, most recently, for the young and edgy *New York*. The establishment was hardly what I wanted to be part of, and I vowed not to regard myself as such.

By the time the family/style editor, Joan Whitman, called me at *New York*, asking me to interview for an opening as a food reporter,

I already had a chip on my shoulder. It dated back to 1972, when Craig Claiborne first retired as food editor. Neither I nor any other female food writer I knew was given an interview for his job, no matter what her credentials. (If any were interviewed, I still would like to hear about it.) Word was out in the food world then that Charlotte Curtis, an ardent feminist and Whitman's predecessor, had been so happy with Craig that she would consider only a man to replace him. (I was told that by Leon Lianides of the Coach House restaurant, who reported hearing it from two loyal customers: Craig Claiborne himself and Theodore Bernstein, the *Times*'s much respected editor and grammarian.) Some of my best friends agreed with Curtis, as did my literary agent over lunch at San Marino ("You've got to admit it's really a man's job . . .") and who did not remain my agent very long after. I almost choked on my stuffed calamari, which I recall as being stale and fishy, although it may have been that I was just swallowing my gall.

When I reported the *Times*'s reluctance to NOW (National Organization for Women), I got what seemed like a patient, noncommittal hearing and no offer of action.

That was the only instance in which I remember feeling discriminated against professionally because of gender, probably because I wrote about food and home furnishings, traditional female provinces, and many women held the top jobs on magazines devoted to them. Apparently restaurant reviewing was different, first because Craig had done it so well but also possibly because a certain cachet was associated with the glamorous reporting of a man-about-town. Or, only God knows what.

I have since come to recognize that men and women generally write differently about food and perhaps about everything else. Men tend to express their opinions in a brasher, more confident or even conceited tone, although those opinions rarely prove more reliable than the carefully couched and subtly appealing assessments made by most women. Men and women usually draw upon different frames of reference, thereby coloring the copy.

In my anger, I sent highly intemperate letters to several editors as well as to the publisher, Arthur Ochs "Punch" Sulzberger. The letter I got back from the managing editor, Peter Millones, who was in charge of editorial personnel, told me in essence that the attitude expressed in my letters indicated that I could never be employable at the *Times*.

Apparently I was the only one who remembered any of this, but I could not resist bringing it up to Abe Rosenthal after two Scotches in his office when he offered me the job. He immediately agreed that I was right to be indignant and that, at the very least, I had deserved an interview. Thus calmed, I decided to go to the *Times*, fighting my reluctance to leave feisty *New York* and join a bunch of elite snobs and have my stories heavily edited, as the *Times*'s copy desks were reputed to do. I was also disturbed that the job did not include being the restaurant critic, a post then held by John Canaday. But Abe assured me it would be mine when Canaday relinquished it, which would occur, he said, not more than eighteen months later. In addition, I ignored Clay Felker's attempt to keep me at *New York* with a warning that the *Times* was in such bad financial shape it would soon be sold to the *Chicago Tribune*.

As it turned out, Clay was not far wrong. The *Times* was indeed in the midst of a financial crisis, and a major battle was in progress between the business heads and the editors. The first wanted to initiate a four-section paper plus suburban supplements instead of the traditional two sections, thereby increasing readership with more soft features and, ultimately, more advertising. The plan was resisted by the editors, Rosenthal foremost among them, who considered soft news lower ground. Although a newcomer, I shared that editorial view, feeling it would make the serious *Times* no better than many out-of-town newspapers with sections dedicated to home furnishings, food, fashion, sports, culture and similar features. As I look back, my view—not that it mattered—was a knee-jerk reaction to being on the side of editorial angels rather than of business devils. My attitude was especially inexplicable because Clay Felker had made me believe in the value of service pieces, a field he pioneered. These pieces gave *New York* its strength when combined with hard news, in-your-face reports on politics, finance and assorted local scandals. I remain convinced that there are more people interested in knowing where to buy the best bagel than about the latest act of political or corporate corruption, primarily because they personally can do something about the bagel but feel powerless against the Enrons of the world.

Years after, when the *Times* special sections were up and running most successfully thanks to the diligence, courage and imagination of Abe Rosenthal, his managing editor and sidekick, Arthur Gelb, and their talented, much overworked staffs, I was asked which editor I thought had made the most difference in the *Times*'s turnaround. Unexpectedly, I found myself answering, "Clay Felker," because he set the paradigm that the *Times* and many other newspapers and city magazines followed.

My worst fears about going to the *Times* were misplaced, especially relating to the staff, I decided after my first week of indoctrination. During that period I spent part of each day touring the production facilities, sitting in at the city, foreign and culture desks and at the daily editorial and front page meetings, all to clue me in on how the impressive system worked. Never, before or since, have I felt so immediately at home with so many strangers. Despite a few inevitably pretentious blowhards, most came across as consummate New Yorkers even if they were not natives—helpful and fast-talking in a lingo I clearly understood—and who behaved with a casual informality that belied what were often impressive accomplishments. I felt as though I had grown up with them, Abe

Rosenthal included. Only a few of the women reporters in the style department to which I was attached (then still referred to as the women's page by most people) were icily aloof and remained so for six or eight months. Their indifference was more than made up for by the supportive friendliness and guidance from Joan Whitman and the instant friendship of Lawrence Van Gelder, then in that department, and who became one of my most loyal Green Beret eaters (that elite clan who were ever at the ready to join me at short notice for any restaurant meal, good or bad), and a little later, the stylish columnist and reporter Enid Nemy, who remains one of my most loyal friends. I also found helpful friends at the culture desk, most especially Marvin Siegel, and Seymour Peck, the savvy and sardonic culture editor who remembered the minutest details of every movie he ever saw and many he had not. Herbert Mitgang, the handsome and literate Lincoln scholar, critic and fellow Brooklynite, kept trying to convince me that airlines' meals in little fitted trays were "cute" and also that the real problem at the *Times* was that the two top editors—Rosenthal and Gelb—came from the Bronx. I quickly came to realize that for sheer fun, nothing matched lunch at some small ethnic restaurant with the late Richard Shepard, whose ear for the soul and humor of the New York street was unmatched and who was always learning new languages. He conversed with the staff in Portuguese at Cabaña Carioca as we dug into clams in green sauce and feijoada, or in Chinese as we ordered throwback Cantonese dishes like chicken subgum, egg rolls and shrimp in lobster sauce in the second-floor New Republic just across from the *Times* building, or Yiddish and Russian-Polish in the Café Edison (a.k.a. the Polish Tearoom), where we restored ourselves with cold borscht, blintzes, potato pancakes, lox and eggs and all manner of rolls and coffee cakes.

My fear of being heavily edited also was groundless. Editors and the copy desk often made minor changes, requested a different

lede—spelled that way so the production department did not con-
fuse it with the instruction to lead, or add more space between the
lines—or trimmed copy, since I always wrote too much. These
changes were never made without my knowledge and were often
improvements. Sure, there were occasional battles when I refused
to make some changes just to exercise that prerogative.

I never felt any pressure to please or go easy on stories that
would affect advertisers. Shortly after my arrival, I was invited to a
luncheon in the *Times*'s corporate dining room, where various editors hosted executives of a supermarket chain. It was one of a
series of such off-the-record lunches held as background for
reporters covering a particular field. I later told Abe Rosenthal that
I felt uncomfortable being a participant at off-the-record proceedings and he told me in a most friendly way that I would not have to
do so again.

I also met no objection to my proposal for a story that Clay
Felker had not let me do at *New York*: a blind tasting by several
qualified staff members of private label liquors made for certain
bygone retail outlets, comparing them to the largest-selling name
brands in the city. Clay had said it was a great idea but if done
would have to be reported honestly. Knowing that inevitably some
of the private labels would beat the name brands, he declined, saying that liquor was one of his most important categories of advertising and he could not afford to lose any of it. No such concern
was expressed by editors at the *Times*. I held the tastings over a
five-day period in the test kitchen, pressing into service—much
against their wills—Frank Prial, Craig Claiborne and Pierre
Franey, there being enough sinks for each of us to spit into.

We sampled Scotch, bourbon, rye, vodka and gin and, sure
enough, several private labels, such as those of the bygone Ven-
dome liquor store, prevailed, even though they were made by the
brand name producers, it was said, to the stores' specifications.

Coming out two weeks before Christmas, the largest liquor-selling season of the year, the article drew hundreds of customers to the winning stores. A few weeks later I heard that two million dollars' worth of advertising had been canceled. I asked Abe Rosenthal if that was true. He said, "That's none of your business. It was a great story."

Soon after I arrived, the plan for four special sections took shape, with "Weekend" first appearing on April 30, 1976. I wrote a piece on food in jazz clubs called "More Than Just Jam with Your Jazz!" That was the first time that I ever worked with the "Weekend" deputy editor, Marvin Siegel, thereby beginning a long and most worthwhile friendship and working relationship. Marvin is the sort of person who knows everything about New York, the movies, culture and sports, and so he caught many errors and added insights. He was also a gentle but firm copy editor and when I eventually wrote the restaurant reviews that ran in his section, he developed an excellent system for dealing with them. He always read from hard copy even after computers were installed, and he covered up my star rating, then read the text to see if the two coincided. On the rare occasions when he felt they did not, he would "suggest" that I reread my review and decide whether to change the number of stars or the text.

Until the advent of "Weekend," the restaurant reviews appeared on the Wednesday food page and it was there that my first reviews ran, when John Canaday took a four-week vacation. It is hard to believe that the editors allowed me to start with a four-star review of the original Palm, then in its heyday, because it was the first review by a substitute. Rosenthal questioned that, but I convinced him that I was hardly an unknown at the *Times*, having appeared for many months before. He also acquiesced because I had an unusual feature in the review. Never offering customers menus, the Palm waiters recited a few specials to each diner without mentioning price and without letting on how many other choices were available. In my five or six visits preceding the review, I noticed many dishes not offered to us: steak à la Stone (sliced steak topped with sautéed onions and roasted peppers), beef à la Dutch (a sort of stew), chicken Bruno (chopped and fried with lots of garlic) and various pastas among many other culinary secrets. When finished with my visits I called Bruce Bozzi, who with his cousin Wally Ganzi owned the restaurant, and asked if I could print a list of every dish they prepared, with prices, and he complied. It was something of a coup and for years customers pulled out the tattered list of dishes before they ordered.

When Canaday returned, he volunteered to leave the reviewing post ahead of schedule because, he said, I obviously took it much more seriously than he did and deserved it. Joan Whitman and I asked him to keep it for two more months, giving me time to build up a backlog of reviews, and he did so.

That John Canaday filled that post at all had to do with Craig Claiborne's return to the paper in 1974. At the editors' requests, Craig agreed to return on the condition that he would not have to review restaurants, something he understandably detested after fourteen years. Until then, the critic had also written other food articles, as did Craig's short-lived successors, Raymond Sokolov and John Hess. But with Craig back, they needed someone else only to review restaurants, a function that at the time they did not feel warranted a full salary. They wanted a graceful writer interested in food and with a broad international knowledge of it, and so lighted on Canaday, their very urbane art critic.

"It's okay to slap a man in the face, but you don't have to cut his cheek with your ring. Remember, have a little *rachmones . . .*" With that advice, enforced by the Yiddish word for compassion,

Abe Rosenthal anointed me food critic of the *New York Times* in August 1976.

"Let's have a celebration lunch!" suggested Larry Van Gelder. "I say it's hot dogs from Nathan's for all."

It was the perfect choice, not only because I passionately love hot dogs (the closest I come to a junk food predilection) but mostly because the Nathan's Famous branch then on Times Square harked back to my childhood days at the Coney Island original, where I had a prophetic first exercise in concentrated, comparative tasting. To celebrate graduation from elementary school, a group of us were out for a night of rides and carousing, and we began to argue about the relative merits of hot dogs at Nathan's and the nearby Feltman's, where, legend has it, the American hot dog—a frankfurter served on a warm bun—was invented by the owner, Charles Feltman, in the 1870s. Before the evening ended, we had made four round-trips between the two, downing eight specimens each just to be absolutely sure of our verdict. Even if I could remember the winner it would be moot, as Nathan's Famous is the only option still standing, Feltman's having closed in 1954. Yet in that simplistic comparison, I unwittingly began a technique I would resort to when rating loftier fare such as caviar, truffles and cheese as a professional food critic.

We sized up the hot dogs by appearance (bright burnished red and sleek, not gray-brown or wrinkled), aroma (fresh and spicy, not stale or sour), texture (meaty, tender and snappily juicy, not mealy, dry or rubbery), flavor (smoky beef, peppery and garlicky) and after-flavor (no bitter or medicinal lingerings). For the sake of purity, we tried them with and without rolls and mustard. (Ketchup and relish were never authentic dressings for a New York wiener and I don't recall Nathan's or Feltman's ever serving sauerkraut.)

Despite my earlier experiences as a restaurant critic, I felt a special burden descend upon me, awed as I was by the *Times*'s reputation for seriousness and because of its power, which put much at stake for both restaurant owners and customers. I was clear about my main allegiance being to the public, but I also wanted to give owners a fair shake; I not only followed the *Times*'s rule about a three-visit minimum before writing a restaurant review but often went six or eight times and in one case twelve, just to be sure.

In the seven and a half years that followed, the reviews I most enjoyed were those in which I reported on very good restaurants not generally in the public eye, none more so than the one in which I gave three stars to Rao's on August 19, 1975. A tiny corner bar in Spanish Harlem, formerly an Italian neighborhood, Rao's had eight tables and a clientele that included mobsters, journalists, sports figures and assorted neighborhood types who hung around the bar in undershirts. Dick and I were introduced to it by our friend and local Democratic New York state assemblyman, William F. Passannante, who wisely introduced me as Mrs. Falcone. Looking much as it does now with its year-round Christmas decorations and photos of celebrity patrons on the walls, it was run by chef-owner Vincent Rao, who cooked wearing a ten-gallon hat, and his wife, Anna, always an immaculate vision in starchy whites. The food, Italian-American classics such as seafood salad, meatballs, pastas, lemon chicken and sausages and peppers, was sublime and I wanted to write about the place.

After my third visit, I announced myself, and Frank Pellegrino, nephew of the owner and the manager of the dining room, said it would be all right for me to write a few lines. I said that I would write as many lines as I wanted to and did. The result was that Rao's telephone rang off the walls to such an extent that a few callers were told where they could go, and eventually, the receiver was taken off the hook. Feeling this would all blow over after their August vacation, the Raos and Frank were surprised—and, ultimately, delighted—that it did not.

Shortly after the review appeared, I had a call from Lt. David Durk, of the New York City Police Department, reminding me of his book, *The Pleasant Avenue Connection,* written with Ira J. Silverman and Arlene Durk. It was a novel based on his work as an undercover detective investigating organized crime and he pointed out that Rao's used to be the site for "mob sit-downs," where matters of vital importance were decided, a sort of raffish credential, I thought. Such activities hardly drive the public away as proven recently when a customer shooting at Rao's brought a renewed flood of requests for reservations. I even teased Frank Pellegrino about having staged it to renew luster to the restaurant's increasingly tame reputation.

I always resisted the temptation to keep a few choice finds for myself by not reviewing them, preferring to get credit for the discovery.

Another review I counted as a triumph was the four-star rating I gave to Vienna '79, a suave, modern Austrian restaurant on East 79th Street. I had not heard about it until a year after it opened, but the food was so elegantly and lightly rendered yet full of authentic flavors, all in a stunning setting devoid of the usual Vienna Woods kitsch, that I felt it deserved the rating. I never made the automatic judgment that one ethnic cuisine was categorically better than any other and tried to approach each visit to each restaurant as though I had never been there before, totting up the score for all visits at the end. To be fair, on a first visit I regarded every restaurant as eligible for four stars and even awarded them to Hatsuhana when it was new and innovative and prepared the most impeccable sushi.

Star ratings were the subject of intermittent debates as they were used in no other criticism at the *Times.* It was begun by Craig Claiborne, following the Michelin tradition. For a while I agreed with those who thought it childish, finding it annoying to deal with and feeling that readers should make their own judgments after reading

the reviews. Also, when a rating was low, many would skip the
review altogether, thereby missing details that might have proven
interesting. I soon changed my mind, first because readers seem to
love seeing stars, but also because they represent an instant, reduc-
tive score. If the ratings are decent, restaurateurs like them, too, as
an easy way to succinctly report an accolade in an advertisement or
in a window. More important, however, I came to realize that by
having to reduce my opinions to an exact score made me more dili-
gent about deciding how I truly felt.

One startling event took place when all of New York law
enforcement was searching for the Son of Sam killer. I received a
call from the Queens district attorney asking if I had ever known
or heard of a suspect who had escaped from the Creedmore psychi-
atric facility and who had left behind a manila folder full of my
restaurant reviews. He had worked in the kitchen of a restaurant in
the TWA terminal at Kennedy Airport and may have had bigger
things in mind. I said I had never heard of him and promised to call
the D.A.'s office if I did.

My only regret about my experience at the *Times* was Craig
Claiborne's falling out with me. Craig did more to bring the word
of good food to this country than any other writer, and he wrote
stories about famous chefs from various restaurants in his well-
outfitted test kitchen in the Hamptons. Several times, quite coincidentally, I gave negative reviews to some of those chefs shortly
before or after his stories appeared. Craig stopped speaking to me
entirely, accusing me of putting down his taste. I was distressed that
he believed that, as I did not think he was necessarily wrong to
praise the chefs I'd criticized. In his own kitchen, they'd undoubtedly cooked superbly, while giving short shrift to unknowns in their
restaurants.

"Aren't your reviews very subjective?" I have often been asked
in a somewhat accustory tone. The answer is, "You betcha . . . and

how!" If I qualify or expand on that answer, it is usually with "they are objectively subjective," meaning I reported only what *I* thought—my opinion—without modifying it to include outside influences. To do so, I tried not to read other critics' reviews about places I had not been to, or to listen to the opinions of anyone else at my table, a practice that would be tantamount to a theater critic running up and down the aisles asking the audience what they thought. Most of all, I avoided socializing with other restaurant critics, not wanting to digest their opinions.

One of the accusations I had to field most often came when a new restaurant received a bad review. "You don't understand our problems. You reviewed us too soon," was the standard gist of unfavorably reviewed restaurants' complaints.

In fact, because of my work with Restaurant Associates, I did understand their problems but did my best to ignore them—they were not the concern of a public paying top dollar. (I have often wanted to explain to them my problems as a writer—all that typing, punctuation, grammar, spelling!) As for reviewing an establishment too soon, my feeling is that as soon as a restaurant is open and full prices are being charged it is fair game. In practice, it was not possible to make the required visits before a month went by, so rarely did a review appear earlier.

One review that caused a brief run-in with Abe Rosenthal came after I wrote a fairly negative review of the newly opened, wildly extravagant Tavern on the Green produced in true Hollywood fashion by the late Warner LeRoy. He complained to Abe that I was harder on him than I would have been on an unknown novice and that I reviewed his restaurant too soon after it opened.

Abe, Joan Whitman and I met in her office and he read LeRoy's complaint. He asked if I would have been as hard on a small restaurant I found disappointing after someone had recommended it to me. I answered that if it were an obscure restaurant and not good,

I would not review it at all. What was the point of telling people not to go to a place they had never heard of? I also added that because of the mass of publicity about Tavern, readers were calling to find out if it was good. "Now, that's a perfect answer," he said. "You mean Tavern was a matter of public interest." And that's what he told LeRoy.

He also stood by me when another restaurateur began a letter complaining about a negative review with the opener "I am a survivor of the Holocaust" and tipped Abe Rosenthal off about his restaurant critic having written a pornographic piece for the autumn 1962 issue of *Eros*, which became a collector's item because it contained the last studio photographs of Marilyn Monroe, taken by Bert Stern six weeks before her death. Abe searched it out, read it and told me, "That may be the most interesting story you've ever written." What he did not know is that I had written others for Ginzburg under pseudonyms.

Not all of my experiences at the *Times* were equally delightful.

Shortly after the debut of the Wednesday food section, which required much more editorial assistance than we were staffed to provide, Craig, Pierre and I felt we were drowning in work. I wanted another writer for the department, a part-time secretary to help with correspondence and gathering material for my reviews and a significant raise. When I approached James Greenfield, the managing editor in charge of our department, he refused all requests. I asked other editors, threatening to quit, and got the same answer, namely, that they would not be bullied. I then made a cold call to Rupert Murdoch to see if he was interested in having me write for both *New York* and the *New York Post* and he gave me an appointment the very next day. We met in his office, then down on South Street, and made a lot of headway before he had his limousine take me back to the *Times*, where I announced that I would be leaving. Jimmy Greenfield was furious and told me to clear out of the office immediately as he threw away about one hundred loaves of bread I had collected for a story.

I made a tentative deal with James Brady, then the editor of *New York,* on a Friday. But on Saturday I had a call from Peter Millones, saying he was just back from vacation and was sorry about the turn things took and would I compromise on any of my demands. I said I would not and through the weekend there were a series of calls with the *Times* upping the offer and me standing fast. Finally, late on Sunday afternoon, Millones called and asked, "If we give you everything you want, will you come in tomorrow morning and pretend nothing ever happened?" I agreed and did, the only awful part being that I had to suffer Jim Brady's wrath because he felt he had been played.

My next confrontation occurred over computers, something I refused to use longer than almost anyone else, with the exception of a remarkable old metro reporter, Peter Kihss, who worked on a manual typewriter for as long as he was there. Writing was (and is) hard enough for me without having to get used to new mechanics, and because the typographers forced a rule that unless a reporter typed his or her own copy into the system, it would have to be done by a member of the union—a way to save jobs. So I called my stories into the phone room, which was still allowed for reporters in the field. Mine, however, usually came from home, where I had to spell out all foreign and obscure words. I became overconfident and began calling the phone room from my desk at the *Times.* Thus was I defeated by a canny operator who somehow didn't believe me and called the home number I had given her. Getting neither a busy signal nor an answer, she realized I was elsewhere. That provoked a mad screaming session between Jimmy Greenfield and me, friends though we were and are, and only the classy, civilized reasoning of managing editor Seymour Topping convinced me at least to try using a computer. Now I wonder how I ever stood using the typewriter, which required making about ten carbons for each story and correcting them neatly.

In his recent memoir, *City Room*, Arthur Gelb recounts an event about the first time I quit. In his version, he has confused two separate incidents. Although as I have said, there was never any pressure to favor advertisers or friends, and only occasionally and in fun did Arthur "Punch" Sulzberger or Abe Rosenthal say as we met in the hall or elevator, "Well, I guess I can't show my face in '21' (or L'Aiglon or Sardi's) anymore," the one person who did try to have many critics favor friends was Gelb. And if a critic in any field gave a negative review, Gelb was known to assign other reporters to features that would make it up to the victim. He also astonished me once when I suggested a story rating the ten top butchers in New York. He thought it was a great idea but insisted that I should include all boroughs and suburbs where they were hoping to expand circulation. I explained that it would be impossible; Manhattan alone would be a huge job, to which he answered, "Can't you get some names from the Yellow Pages?"

But the final argument that convinced me to leave concerned the review of Alfredo's, a pricey Italian restaurant that was a big favorite with Gelb and Rosenthal, on Central Park South where San Domenico now stands. It had once been good enough to earn two stars from me. But when I began to collect my reviews for my city restaurant guide published in 1982, I found that I had given many ratings too long ago to be valid so I returned to those places, Alfredo's included. What I found was dreary food and matching service, so bad that one night Dick and I watched a customer leave without paying the check when he could not get the captain's attention and no one noticed but us. Also, Alfredo's appeared regularly in the Sunday paper under a listing of special interest restaurants gathered from past reviews and, of course, with two stars. The only solution both for my book and the column was to review it again in the *Times*, which I did, giving it no stars and a "Fair" rating.

Two nights later, Gelb, having read my copy, called me at home, saying that Abe was angry at me and felt that I wanted to show my independence by giving a bad review to a place the bosses went to. Gelb asked that I raise the rating to at least one star or drop the review and substitute something else. When I refused to do either, he said Abe wanted to see me the very next morning. When I went into Abe's office and explained why I was there, he waved me away with "Get out of here and go back to work." Good cop, bad cop was in fact a game the Gelb-Rosenthal team famously played.

But Gelb never forgot and ordered a story from Craig Claiborne on his favorite neighborhood restaurants in New York, where Craig kept a pied-à-terre in the Osborne apartments, a short walk from Alfredo's, which he included in the story. When I asked Pierre Franey if Craig really liked that restaurant, he said no, but that Gelb had pleaded with him to include it, reminding Craig of the many favors he had done for him. He later ordered up a few other similar stories and made some insulting remarks about me when I was not there, reported by friends who were. I suddenly decided that if that was success, I would try failure, and so I quit in a note to Abe. He must have been relieved, because he immediately announced my resignation in one of the *Times*'s columns. Only after I had signed generous contracts with *Time* and *Vanity Fair* did he ask me to reconsider and stay, but it was too late.

A few days before I was to leave, Abe made a last effort to try to get me to stay, warning, "In six months, it's going to be 'Mimi Who?'" To which I replied, "You just better make sure this paper doesn't become 'the *New York What?*'"

Fortunately we were both wrong.

Don't Call Me Mimi

"WHEN A CRITIC SHOWS UP UNEXPECTEDLY AT A restaurant and is recognized, what can the chef do to improve the food on such short notice?" The short answer is, "Just about everything."

And that's why I became obsessed with preserving my anonymity for as long as I possibly could. Any food professional like a chef, a restaurateur or a food writer who claims that little can be done is either a fool or a liar: a fool because he or she cannot know very much about cooking techniques. More likely, such a person is a liar who is loath to admit otherwise because that would make his or her job less pleasurable or, perhaps, even impossible if a publication cannot afford such costly research and so allows its critic to accept free meals. (My expenses ran about $95,000 in 1983, my last year at the *Times*.)

The longer I reviewed restaurants, the more I became convinced that the unknown customer has a completely different experience from either a valued patron or a recognized food critic; for all practical purposes, they might as well be in different restaurants.

Although legendary after only three years in existence, Le Cirque, in its original home in the Mayfair Hotel, received just two stars in 1974 from one of my predecessors, but its standing as a celebrity circus under the direction of owner Sirio Maccioni was out of proportion to its respectable rating for food. Judged by the gossip column names who gathered daily to blow air kisses and stuff their pockets with petits fours before leaving, it might have rated an entire constellation of its own. Shortly after I joined the *Times*, but six months before I became the restaurant critic, Pierre Franey took me to lunch at Le Cirque and introduced me to Maccioni and his then chef-partner, Jean Vergnes.

Eighteen months later, I safely slipped passed Sirio, Vergnes and the effusively corny, croupier-like maître d', Joseph, eagle-eyed for celebrities but blind to unprepossessing interlopers. In the course of about six visits, I was subjected not only to meals that ranged from very good to merely passable, with a watery sauce on the house's famed spaghetti primavera (snobbishly off the menu and so ordered only by the in crowd), duck that tasted of stale grease, lamb delivered well done when ordered rare, oversalting of everything and grainy soufflés.

The real travesties were the service and general treatment: seating us at cramped corner tables near the kitchen door, even though many others were available; keeping early arriving guests at the bar until our party was complete (forgiveable only in an inexpensive restaurant where turnover is crucial); and on one occasion, seating friends before we arrived and then putting us at a different table where we waited for thirty minutes before discovering Joseph's carelessness or, really, his lack of interest. Pepper mills and cheese graters were not offered to us, nor were nightly specials—the glowing, roseate red mullets, the fragrant white truffles—incredibly enough shown to regulars seated right next to us as though we did not exist. At the last dinner, when the captain presented the dessert wagon, he called out, "What kinda pastry do you want, lady?"

Reducing Le Cirque to one star in August 1977, I earned kudos from many who had shared my fate and brickbats from its most vocal fans as well as from Sirio, who complained to Franey and Craig Claiborne, but to no avail.

Le Cirque was not the only blatant example of why a critic should remain unknown. One evening at the Four Seasons restaurant, where I expected to be recognized, our guests arrived twenty or twenty-five minutes ahead of us as prearranged. Also according to plan, after a few minutes, they ordered appetizers of smoked salmon and pâté. Just as the captain started to slice a dried-out tail end of salmon on the tableside gueridon, Dick and I arrived. Recognizing us, the captain spun the cart toward the kitchen, returning a few minutes later with a whole new side of salmon that he began to slice—in the choice middle, yet—as he greeted us. "Good evening, Miss Sheraton, Mr. Falcone . . . Nice to see you here."

"Especially nice for our friend who ordered the salmon," I answered.

Through the years, fresh breads and cakes replaced stale ones at several places when I appeared even if it was too late in the evening for new cakes to be cut. Wilted floral centerpieces were replaced by brighter blossoms. Once, I spotted the homemade tortellini I had ordered being carried into a new East 58th restaurant from its sister restaurant with its older, superior kitchen across the street. *Fatta in casa* indeed, but in which *casa*?

But none of these top the abysmal experiences I encountered at Régine's, which I rated "Poor" in January 1982. We arrived on a Saturday night for a second anonymous visit to this bustling New York branch of the Parisian supper club directed by the henna-haired social dominatrix, Régine. Euro-trash and local climbers could hardly wait to get in. It took weeks to wrest an eight o'clock reservation for this busiest night. The reservation was in the name of Mr. Lawrence, as in Lawrence Van Gelder. Steering us through the jam-packed room, the maître d' acknowledged the reservation but sighed, "Oh, I don't know where I'm going to seat you. We are inundated with royalty tonight!" Then, in an aside to a captain he whispered, "The king will be here at midnight with six body-guards . . ."

Not a very popular king, I thought with glee, realizing that great copy was in the making. We were inched over to a tiny table where two of us were seated in the aisle so that our chairs would be kicked rhythmically by the passing parade. What followed was agoniz-ingly slow and distracted service and food that included over-the-hill shellfish, rubbery quenelles, acrid duck pâté and pastry with the texture of Uneeda biscuits. On this and two other visits I ordered a soufflé and each time was given the extraordinary excuse that the soufflé oven was not working. Recalling the ritual four questions asked at the Passover seder, I thought of a fifth: "Where-fore is a soufflé oven different from all other ovens?" Or could it possibly be that the kitchen didn't want to bother making soufflés for unimportant guests? At the end of the evening, our captain asked if dinner had been satisfactory and when we indicated it was not, he shrugged and said, "Well, you can't fight City Hall!"

At a lunch one day when the captain ignored me and two women friends, we, in desperation, ordered desserts from a waiter. When he failed to deliver, we caught the captain's eye only to be told, "If Madame knew how to order properly from a captain instead of from a waiter, perhaps she would get things promptly."

I was often assured by many in the field that such reviews taught New York restaurateurs a lesson and that service had improved and, skeptical though I tried to be, as I gradually became known I almost was convinced of that. But proof that little had changed came by way of Ruth Reichl's first review of Le Cirque in the *New York Times* in 1993, shortly after she became the third critic to follow me. Her report of meals at Le Cirque, before and after being known, seemed to echo many of my long-ago experiences at that restaurant and Régine's, complete with references to royalty.

I do hope that one consideration shown to a known critic is now available to all who need it, and that is the treatment and acceptance of the handicapped. One of our dear family friends, long confined to a wheelchair, who with her husband was warmly welcomed and royally treated at the many European restaurants they frequented, occasionally dined with us, always producing grimaces from the managements until I appeared. At one bygone restaurant, no one attempted to unlock revolving doors so that the wheelchair could easily pass through, and both friends were awkwardly waiting outside as I arrived. They reported that several restaurants in New York even had claimed that wheelchairs were against the city fire laws and so all four of us ate at those restaurants together, asking if that was true, to which all replied that it was not.

The instances of a chef or a manager doing nothing special for recognized critics are few, limited to those practitioners who think they are doing everything right, or to others impervious to reviews. Those in the know were always extra polite, served larger portions of the best cuts, kept busboys refilling water glasses after every sip and surrounded us with enough servers to perform a heart transplant. In a few old-style Italian restaurants, mushrooms—apparently symbols of elegance—were heaped over everything.

Salt was another giveaway. I preferred not to have chefs gratuitously protecting my health and often faulted kitchens for under-salting. When I was recognized, therefore, my food often was so bitingly salty that I returned it, undoubtedly causing the chefs to wonder if I really knew my own mind and palate. Some were reported to complain to colleagues, "First she says there is not enough salt, then that there is too much." Exactly!

When food is cooked to order, much can be done with it and often is, especially at the expensive, trendy establishments. But even in the least expensive Chinese restaurants, cooks can choose only the best ingredients properly cut, and stir-fry them in a well-cleaned wok with fresh rather than re-used oil, then add authentic seasonings not tempered to the American palate, all big steps toward curing the most common flaws in presenting that cuisine. That last consideration about authentic seasoning applies not only to hot and spicy seasonings in Hunan, Sichuan, Mexican and Indian dishes but to garlic in Italian food, lard in German and some American dishes, cilantro and lemongrass in Southeast Asian specialties and more.

In addition, all fish, poultry and meats that are not prepared in advance can be cooked as ordered—rare, medium or well-done. Such requests accounted for some of the longest waiting periods I suffered when recognized, as, for example, a steak accidentally done past my requested rare being served to another diner, while a second was started on the grill for me. The much hyped but long-gone Palace on East 59th Street, known more for its high prices than for its excellence, had an ostentatious Louis-the-Last decor reminiscent of better dress departments in Saks Fifth Avenue and Neiman Marcus. It was two years old and still a hot topic when I reviewed it in 1977, and I invited the *Times*'s wine writer, Frank Prial, and his wife, Jean, to join us, so that he could critique the wine list. On this, my second visit, we were made from the start and were accorded lavish service except for the inexplicable hour-and-a-half wait between a fish course and the roasted duck with green pepper-corn sauce I ordered. Months later I learned from a former kitchen worker that it had taken three ducks to get one cooked to the rosy-red, medium-rare perfection deemed suitable for me. True to the restaurant's reputation for high prices, my check was relatively the biggest I have ever racked up—about $850—primarily because during the duck-induced pause, Prial tiptoed through and ordered from the pricey, exceptional wine list.

Even on short notice much can be done to improve many pre-pared dishes shortly before they are served if the chef deems it nec-essary for a critic or a highly prized client. Soups and the gravies or sauces of stews and braised meats can be thinned or thickened and their seasonings corrected, while more of better ingredients can be added (like clams to clam chowder), or a fresh vegetable garnish prepared. With any sort of meatloaf or pâté, dried end slices can be eliminated (as with the Four Seasons salmon), or they might be served to unknowns, or whole loaves can be started if the cut ones have been around too long. In extreme circumstances, say, when a dish is scorched or otherwise beyond repair, the critic may be told that the last portion has been sold—hard to believe when it occurs at a 12:30 lunch, as it once did.

In 1984, when I wrote on this subject for *Vanity Fair*, I received a call from Adi Giovanetti, the proprietor of the prominent Il Nido. "Signora, you don't know the half of it," he said. "There is a lot more that we can do, especially if you order an appetizer. That gives us plenty of time to fix the main course."

For these reasons and more, and following examples set by the Guide Michelin and my predecessors at the *Times*, I tried to remain anonymous. And fueled by the romantic notion of undercover agents in disguise, I believe I was the first restaurant critic to collect a wardrobe of wigs. One was an auburn pageboy affair with straight bangs that I dubbed the Greenwich Village Lady Poet.

A second, the Five Towns Macher, was done up as a silver-blond bouffant cascading over one eye. The third was a long, loose, comb-down of black hair that partially obscured my face in the style of an anguished activist, perhaps more Mimi Montag than Susan Sontag. I usually went to dinner directly from the *Times* or from my home and, not wanting colleagues or neighbors to know what my disguises looked like, I awkwardly donned them in taxis with only a small purse mirror to check results.

Despite perfect eyesight, I bought several pairs of eyeglasses, accessories no one associated with my face. I had them fitted with nonprescription lenses that were tinted, the better to obscure my glance as I studied the room. That last was a lesson I learned during a breakfast at Lou Mitchell's in Chicago's financial district, where this super coffee shop attracts early-bird workers from the mercantile and stock exchanges. Standing on the long waiting line, I tried to figure out the pattern of action. After a few minutes the manager approached, offering me the little box of Milk Duds distributed to ladies-in-waiting and asked, "So where is your place?" When I looked confused at the question, he continued, "I figure you must be in the business because of the way your eyes are working the room."

I made reservations in fictitious names or in those of friends dining with us. When the names were totally fake, I sometimes forgot which I used. Dick and I overcame that touchy situation by expressing embarrassment at the desk and apologizing for not being able to recall who we were dining with and suggesting that a peek at the reservation book would help. The ploy always worked, although it made us appear to be having a precocious senior moment.

Sometimes I paid for meals with the credit cards of dining companions, but usually I paid in cash, necessitating thrice weekly advances from the *Times* cashier, who always seemed grumpy at my requests, as though I was profligate with his money. At first, such advances were always in twenty-dollar bills, creating large bundles and a suspicious modus operandi, so I began placing advance orders for different denominations. At first I feared that paying cash would be a giveaway, but I needn't have worried; it was (and remains) a fairly common way to hide unreported income, both for customers and those restaurateurs who might be so inclined.

That is why I still resent and avoid places where only cash is accepted, unless, of course, as in Chinatown, where the prices are too low to cover the fees required by credit card companies. One very savvy New York restaurateur, now deceased, charged modestly high prices and did a wildly successful cash-only business, but he quickly closed a newer branch in an Atlantic City hotel because the rent was a percentage of the gross and had to be backed up with credit card receipts. "I can't make out well enough if I have to pay credit card fees *and* all of the taxes, too," he complained indignantly.

Fellow diners were warned not to call me Mimi, with Clara or Louise suggested as substitutes, because I feared a staff member might be alert to that name, if to nothing else. Alas, the few incurable Mimi-sayers were never invited again. Intermittently, word would get back to me that some lay diners deliberately used that name for precisely the reasons I avoided it. There were even more brazen types who used to call in my name for a hard-to-get reservation and to receive special treatment, and some who, once there, announced they were me or my assistant, hoping for a free meal. A few wisely suspicious restaurateurs knew I did all of my own eating and called the *New York Times* operator (who would not give out staff telephone numbers), asking that I call them so that they could check on the imposters.

One such attempt at securing a difficult reservation was made by my cousin, the painter and art dealer Wallace Reiss. Knowing I would not ask for special consideration on anyone's behalf, he called asking for a table at Le Cygne right after I gave it four stars, announcing that he was my cousin. "That's what they all say, monsieur," was the answer he got, and deserved. A great cook and a passionate food lover, Wally and his wife, Irene, sometimes accompanied us on review forays. Inevitably, as we approached the entrance he would whisper, "I hope they recognize you so we get great food."

Evidence of similar chicanery was rarely more telling than at a charming little Cuban restaurant on Cornelia Street in Greenwich Village, run by a young American woman who had studied that cuisine. Our companions that evening were two of our closest friends and most experienced Green Berets, Shirley and Sidney Cohlan, both pediatricians who, it often seemed, took care of every child in New York, our son included. Sure enough, when we entered the restaurant they realized that the chef-owner had been their patient. Not wanting to blow my cover, or to be rude, they introduced us as Mr. and Mrs. Anderson. I decided that I would use the advantage to get a line on the owner and I asked how business was.

"Oh, just great," she said, "and it's going to get much better. Last week, Mimi Sheraton was here."

"Really?" I answered. "That must have been exciting for you. Was she nice? Did she like the food?"

"Very nice," she answered, "but of course she doesn't make up her mind until she has been at least three times, and then you don't know until you read the review."

Happy that she at least had some details correct, I made two subsequent visits as Mrs. Anderson, then gave the restaurant two stars.

When the owner called to thank me, I departed from my practice of not revealing myself even after a review appeared, in case I had to return or encountered the owner or a staff member in another restaurant.

"Do you remember the night the Cohlans came in for dinner?" I asked. "I was with them when you said I had been in the week before. What made you think that other woman was me?"

"My press agent brought her and introduced her as you. I pay him based on the number of press people he brings in," she answered.

"If I were you I would fire him," I advised.

At another dinner at Il Cortile on Mulberry Street in Little Italy, James Greenfield was dining with friends who knew the owner. When they introduced Jimmy as being at the paper, the owner said, "You must recognize the woman sitting two tables behind you . . ."

Looking around, Jimmy said he did not.

"Oh, you just don't want us to know . . . It's Mimi Sheraton."

"I see her every day and I swear to you that is not Mimi Sheraton," Jimmy reported saying, doubting that he was believed.

Confusion about my identity resulted in other amusing occurances, none more so than at a sushi restaurant near the *Times* building. Since my reviews were submitted on Tuesdays for the Friday "Weekend" section, where they then appeared (and still belong), Abe Rosenthal, the executive editor, looked for the chance to beat the crowds to a top-rated place, especially for Japanese or Indian food, cuisines he had acquired a taste for as a foreign correspondent in those countries. Seeing a two-star review for this nearby sushi outpost, he made a reservation as always, saying it was for the editor of the *New York Times*. When he arrived, his greeting from the owner was, "Ah, Mimi Sheraton, we are happy to have you here." Nothing he said could dissuade the smiling, bowing staff, who apparently did not recognize Mimi as a female name, and so addressed him by my name for the entire evening despite his efforts to make it clear that he was *the* editor, A. M. Rosenthal, and that Mimi Sheraton was, *merely,* the restaurant critic and a woman. He was at my desk by ten the next morning, laughing over the tale, but not without a certain smirk of resentment at his own name ringing no bells.

I paid high prices for anonymity. I turned down invitations to all events, business or social, if anyone connected to a restaurant or a related establishment was expected. Among the great parties I missed out on were the Christmas galas given by my good friend and colleague Enid Nemy, because Elaine Kaufman (Elaine's) and Faith Stewart Gordon (the Russian Tea Room), had accepted, as had a few press agents. Recognition was not the only reason for such avoidances. I felt uncomfortable—almost duplicitous—at the thought of being socially affable with someone to whom I might have to give a negative review.

And at a considerable detriment to the sales of my books, I was never undisguised on television nor did I make any personal appearances such as book signings. I wore the cliché wide-brimmed hat for rare television appearances or for a photograph on a dust jacket or to accompany an article about me. Like other female critics, I never wore such hats to restaurants as they would surely have been tip-offs.

Few things embarrassed me more than being recognized in disguise, feeling idiotic as some captain said, "Good evening, Miss Sheraton." I always debated whether to go into the ladies and, à la Superman, revert to my real self (whichever one of me that might be), or just sit there feeling silly, steaming under the wig. One of the worst of such experiences came in December 1982, when Dick and I went with three friends to the newly opened Water Club overlooking the East River. It was the newest restaurant opened by Michael "Buzzy" O'Keefe, whose River Cafe in Brooklyn had

received a less than glowing review from me, sparking much rant-
ing and raging from him. Having had a successfully anonymous
first visit at his new outpost, I expected no trouble this second time.
The wine we ordered arrived, but no menus. Finally we asked for a
second bottle, but still no menus came. Instead, the manager
arrived, accusing, "We have reason to believe there is a food critic
at this table, and we are not ready to serve critics yet."

As *Times* editors, lawyers and I had agreed, I was never to lie in
answer to a direct question about my identity. I also knew that
under existing innkeepers' laws, a restaurateur or hotelier can
refuse service for any reason—drunkenness, dress, bad behavior—but not because of race, sex or religion. So after a few words
of protest we asked for a check for our wine, but were told there
would be none. Dick answered that we would not leave that
table—not that night or any other time—until we had a check.
And so we paid, taking the almost full second bottle with us.

Recognizing a column item when he created one, O'Keefe or
one of his staff called the *New York Post,* and the very next morning—a Saturday—news of my ouster appeared on Page Six, the
gossip column. "Restaurant boots 'Times' critic," it read. It being a
slow news day, the item went out on a wire service and was picked
up by many newspapers around the country, evoking much controversy in the trade press and a full-page story in *Time* and great
publicity for me. I also received a call from a law professor at the
Cornell University Hotel School, offering to test that old innkeepers' law, as he did not think it would hold up. Several other lawyers
offered to do the same, but, after discussion, *Times* executives
wisely decided that at best ours would be a Pyrrhic victory, for my
identity would surely be blown during a court case. But they
vowed that if this practice was repeated by other restaurateurs, we
would indeed test the waters. (In fact, I remember being refused
service only one other time, in 1986 after I had left the *Times* and

was writing for *Vanity Fair*. In an article, "The Ten Most Over-rated Restaurants in America," I cited the much-lauded Quilted Giraffe, operated by Barry and Susan Wine and then in its second home in New York. About a year later, an out-of-town friend wanted to have lunch there, but when we arrived shortly after two P.M., Susan Wine told the maître d' to say that there would never be a table for me at the restaurant. As recalled recently by Barry Wine, he and his former wife were not only angry at my negative comments that included a restrained original two-star review in the *Times,* but as the hour was late and they had a staff meeting under way, they felt justified in rejecting me.)

Because I had not made the obligatory three visits to the Water Club, I published only a footnote to my regular column in January 1983, describing my one meal when unrecognized as being just fair and recounting the adventures of the second. When called to ask if he would have served a critic who had given the River Cafe a favorable review, O'Keefe told me, "The person I really do want to keep out is you. But to be legal about it, I guess I have to keep out any critic I recognize, at least for the foreseeable future."

Some articles and reviews provoked lawsuits, all of which to my knowledge ended inconclusively—or at least the managements did not let me in on the outcome, although none went to trial. One of the most serious was brought by McDonald's before I was at the *Times* and I wrote a cover story for *New York* magazine, titled "The Burger That's Eating New York," a piece on neighborhoods shunning the entry of the chain into their backyards. Years later I met the legal counsel for McDonald's, who told me that what stung them most was my description of their milk shakes as "aerated Kaopectate."

And at the *Times,* a longtime, self-appointed foe, Pat Cetta of Sparks Steak House, filed suit when I gave his new restaurant on East 46th Street a cool review, in which I not only disliked some of the food but mistakenly described his genuine wood wall paneling as "pseudo," for which we published a correction. Cetta had nursed a wound since my *New York* magazine days, when I wrote that the Palm was my favorite steak house. At the time, Cetta had stormed into the office of publisher Jack Thomas at *New York*, complaining that he was a big advertiser and asking why I was praising the Palm. In the *Times* lawsuit, he claimed that I had a connection with the Palm. In a letter to the *Times*, he threatened to have drivers follow the *Times* delivery trucks to newsstands every Friday, buy up all the copies, and dump them in the Hudson River. We all wished he had, as it would have been a complete sellout.

The last lawsuit at the *Times*, and the one I enjoyed most, which ended in a dramatic fizzle, was brought by a large, glitzy Chinese restaurant, Dish of Salt, in Rockefeller Center. When a somewhat tepid review appeared, their management not only threatened a suit but took a large advertisement in the paper, saying I had never been in their restaurant. Whoever at the *Times* was supposed to clear ads for misrepresentations was decidedly careless that day, and so the ad ran, and was also mounted in the restaurant's huge window. I raised the roof with the *Times*, exhibiting my four itemized register receipts, saying I had worn wigs and glasses and that the last of my four visits was a lunch with Seymour Topping, an old China hand and a *Times* managing editor respected not only for his journalistic prowess but for his unassailable integrity. I said I would sue the paper if they did not publish a correction. At the same time, my own lawyer, the delightfully cool and feisty William M. Borchard, now at Cowan, Liebowitz & Latman, threatened to sue the restaurant if they did not remove the ad from the window immediately, which they did two hours later. The *Times* published a correction, and *Time* magazine reported the story, somewhat gingerly, as Dish was a favorite with many Time-Life staffers.

No wonder, then, that despite denials about paying special attention to critics, restaurant owners went to great pains to find out what I looked like. Some paid high prices for photographs taken before I was a critic and mounted them in the kitchen. That tactic rarely worked because the staff were less alert than the owners, especially at busy hours. Then, too, I no longer looked as I had when the photographs were taken.

As proof there was the memorable evening at impresario George Lang's restaurant Hungaria in the Citicorp Building. We were seated at a table right next to the kitchen door. Each time it swung open, Dick spotted my picture near the exit. Yet no one made the connection, primarily because Lang himself, who knew me well, was not there.

One morning as I left my brownstone house I was startled by a burst of flashbulbs from a car parked at the curb. As the car sped away, I noted the license plate number and, checking it out, found that it had been reported stolen somewhere near Albany, all making for what seems like a silly caper now, but was a bit nerve-shattering at the time.

Some captains and waiters doubled as bounty hunters, gaining prize money from owners for spotting me, a tactic I was totally unaware of until a few years after I left the *Times*. During a dinner in the newly opened Hôtel Plaza Athénée on East 64th Street, a familiar-looking captain greeted me with thanks for having helped pay a year of his son's college tuition.

"I was at Fiorella's on Third Avenue, and you came in many times before reviewing it," he said. "Each time I recognized you, Shelly Fireman gave me two hundred fifty dollars."

"Too bad you didn't let me in on it," I joked. "I would have gone in more often and we'd have split the take."

Among the giveaways to my identity, the most surprising one proved to be my hands. Having demoted La Caravelle from four stars to two in 1978, apparently a much bigger news story than I

expected, I was asked to do an interview on a local television chan-
nel but refused to show my face. Instead, the camera shot my
hands, one holding a pen and a fork. A few weeks later while dining at the original Hubert's restaurant in Brooklyn, I sensed I had
been recognized. The astute and charming owner, the late Karen
Hubert, eventually admitted she recognized my hands and rings
from seeing them on television. Needless to say, there was no pen
in my hand at that table, or at any other, note-taking being a telltale
sign and so strictly forbidden. So was asking for menus in person
(stealing was fine if accomplished discreetly), although my secretary later called for them, arranging a messenger pickup and, usually, she called to check facts.

Sometimes a tip-off would come from a Judas in the guise of a
diner who knew me, including a few so-called friends and even
once, a relative, in attempts to ingratiate themselves with the
house. Other times when I was known in one restaurant, an
employee-hero would call a friend at another nearby to run in and
take a look. That happened in many Chinese restaurants, when a
relative might be waiting tables a block or two away. "Come and
see the Golden Mouth," was the translation of that invitation as
told to me.

It was also in a Chinese restaurant that I unwittingly gave
myself away as a critic by having the six people at my table order
six different soups in individual bowls instead of in large tureens.
When the review ran, the owner called to tell me of my gaffe, saying that it is very rare for more than one kind of soup to be served
to a single group. Fortunately, in any kind of restaurant, diners
tasting each other's food is not suspect, but rather considered the
standard social game, New York Ping-Pong.

Inevitably if gradually, I became recognized where I least wanted
to be—in the high-fashion, highly touted meccas of big spenders,
where, generally, the bridge-and-tunnel crowd, the snobbish pejorative

for those driving in from the suburbs, being regarded as philistines, rarely stood a chance of getting top service or food. That remains especially true on Saturday nights, when the smart set goes to clubs, private parties or country houses, and the top staff, often including the owner and head chef, also take the night off. And so as a reviewer I always dined out on Saturday nights, feeling it most critical to the many readers who needed more help than the rich and famous habitués, who received the special attention they tipped so well for.

It was and is amazing that I managed to remain unknown in as many New York places as long as I did. (It still would be rare, indeed, for me to be recognized outside of Manhattan, with the exception of only a few restaurants in major cities around the country.) Partly that is because I have always kept a low profile, but also because even when unwigged and with little makeup, I tend to blend into the background, an advantage I maintained by not inviting celebrities or exceptional-looking guests to dine with me. Then, of course, there is also a good chance of slipping in unnoticed at many small ethnic restaurants unaware of the review process and its possible effects, and large, sprawling places where there is a high staff turnover, lots of action and no owner or vested manager at the door or in the dining room. I still would be surprised to be recognized, for example, at Tavern on the Green, or in two dozen other high-profile places where no employee would catch on, or in a restaurant too new to have attracted experienced waiters and captains. Fueled by paranoia, I was as often mistaken about thinking I was spotted as when I thought I was not, and so I never gave myself away unless someone openly acknowledged me by name.

Eventually I had to review many places where I became known and in such cases had friends arrive before me, as at the Four Seasons, to ascertain how they were treated and whether they were given the tables requested when the reservation was made. To avoid my voice being recognized, my secretary or Dick or a friend usually made calls, but I often listened in to catch the tone and degree of politeness, accommodation, attitude or arrogance expressed by reservationists. One of my current pet peeves is push-button menu phone systems with music playing as one waits—and waits—and waits, an inhospitable tactic and inexcusable at expensive places where it would behoove the management to spring for real people to answer the telephone as André Soltner did at Lutèce, even at the height of the restaurant's popularity.

Perhaps restaurant owners should follow the lead of the old-fashioned shopkeeper on the Lower East Side who once bragged to me, "We're so nonautomated that we don't even have an answering machine. You call, we talk to you."

I went many more times before rating a restaurant where I was known, hoping to exhaust and subvert attempts to finesse me and, also, to get the full feel of the place and try many dishes repeatedly to judge consistency, and I generally made it plain in the review that I had been recognized. In such instances, there was the danger of my overzealously discounting good service or food because I was known.

"I'd have known it if she was here. She was never in this restaurant," was the message from Michelin three-star French chef Michel Guérard to a visiting American friend and wine writer, shortly after my review of his restaurant, Les Prés d'Eugénie, appeared in the *Times* on June 7, 1978. Perhaps, like the late Alain Chapel of La Mère Charles, who made the same observation, he expected that, like a smoke alarm, lights would flash or a buzzer sound when a food critic crossed the threshold. Funny thing is, with the exception of only a few dishes, those were two of the restaurants I really liked, among the ten Michelin three-star establishments I reported on during that gastronomic tour of France. As usual, however, my few negative comments canceled out all the positives in the minds of chefs and owners.

Subsequently I had friends remind both Guérard and Chapel of our visits, Guérard by mentioning the American couple who caught an overcharge of four hundred francs on their phone bill when checking out of his hotel, and Chapel, who recalled the American couple whose car was stolen from his hotel parking lot, and to whom he generously offered the use of his Mercedes until a replacement came from Avis in nearby Lyon. (We declined, preferring to walk off some calories along the beautiful surrounding farms, where much of Chapel's produce was grown.)

My very mixed rating of Paul Bocuse's establishment outside of Lyon prompted his typically macho verdict that I had an unsatisfactory sex life. What else could possibly account for the fact that I found the decor vulgar, the duck breast tough and salty, and the *gâteau de foies de volailles* tasting as though it had been made of beef liver, instead of the delicate blond livers of Bresse chickens? The late Pierre-Marie Doutrelant, arguably the most objective, literate and candid of French food critics, who wrote for *Le Nouvel Observateur,* told me several years later that the chefs were really stung because the criticisms came not only from an American, but from a woman, or, as one writer in the French magazine *Metro* described me, "a ketchup-slobbering Yankee." *Zut alors!*

I made this one-month *tour de gueule,* then the most lavish the *Times* had ever commissioned, at the height of the nouvelle cuisine craze. The entire American food press had jumped on the bandwagon, agog at the gastronomic miracles created by the young French turks, with nary a negative comment that I ever read, and I read a lot. What seemed obvious was that every writer had been known to the management, evidenced by interviews quoting chefs who testified to their own genius. Yet past experiences in Paris at dismally disappointing culinary landmarks like La Tour d'Argent, Lasserre and Le Grand Véfour made me doubt that all eighteen of *les trois étoiles*, classic or nouvelle, really deserved the same top ratings.

Disguises not being necessary for me in France, my only subterfuge was the name for reservations, all of which I made by phone from New York. I planned a lunch and dinner at each of ten places, to be followed the next year by reports on the remaining eight, in between eating at humbler spots and walking through food markets and museums. That anonymity served a purpose in France at least as much as in the States was proven irrefutably by the findings. Some experiences at places such as the Auberge de l'Ill in Alsace and Pic in Valence were sublime, and almost as good at Guérard's and Chapel's.

The worst was the Oustaù de Baumanière in Les Baux, where travesties such as packaged melba toast, starchy lobster bisque and shriveled lamb chops were served in a tacky setting. The saddest, perhaps, was dinner at the still lauded La Pyramide in Vienne, where in 1953 I had that unforgettable meal overseen by the legendary chef-patron, Fernand Point. Unfortunately, his widow, Mado, had let the place become a shambles with murky food reminiscent of an employee cafeteria, while madame marched through the dining room at two intervals, as mindlessly as an automaton.

Other disappointments included elements at L'Archestrate and Le Vivarois in Paris and at Troisgros in Roanne.

Struck by the inconsistency between my own experiences and the Michelin ratings, and the similarly high rankings accorded by the other two powerful guides, Kleber and Gault-Millau, I decided to try to interview editors to see how ratings were arrived at and how reliable they were. Neither Henri Gault nor Christian Millau agreed to an interview, but I got luckier with the other two.

Jean Didier, then director and editor-in-chief of the Guide Kleber (no longer published), claimed it was understandable that all guides agreed. "We are all French and have a common background and agree on the standards of cuisine."

About Pyramide's decline he said, "Yes, I am aware of what you describe . . . If I follow my head I do one thing. If I follow my heart I do another. Fernand Point was the spiritual father of today's greatest chefs, and his wife is now an old woman. The reason for the top rating is, of course, sentiment." He also hinted that the directors of the various guides felt a responsibility to certain towns that might not attract tourists were there no three-star to draw them, Vienne being a perfect case in point.

"At fifty to sixty dollars per person [1978 prices], perhaps it would be better not to send people there," I suggested. "Maybe a statue in Vienne's park or naming a professional cooking school after Point would be more appropriate."

In what was said to be the first interview a Guide Michelin editor ever granted a journalist, I spoke with a director, M. Aubry, who said, "It is not possible for Pyramide to be so good as it was because Madame Point can longer maintain the consistency . . . No, it is not exactly sentiment—that is a difficult idea . . . We prefer to wait a long time before stars are taken away. We take stars away immediately only if the chef dies or leaves the restaurant."

"Then why not from Pyramide following Point's death?" I asked.

"Because that is an exception. He had trained the chef who succeeded him."

It was this account that not only inflamed the chefs involved, but became hot news in several major French newspapers and magazines, extending to Germany's *Süeddeutsche Zeitung* in a headline that translated to ATLANTIC BATTLE CONCERNING CULINARY PARADISE.

Metro published a letter by Claude Lebey-Jolly (also sent to the entire food establishment in the United States), who wore the hats of both food critic and food publicist, damning the article and me along with it. Several issues of a food broadside, *Opinions Gourmandes,* carried photographs of a nude woman in a pool, whom they called alternately Mimi Hilton and Mimi Holiday Inn, avowing that Mimi Sheraton must be a stripper at the Crazy Horse Saloon.

As a final flourish, I was invited to be a guest on French television's discussion forum, *Dossiers de l'Écran* (Files of the Screen). With me would be the chefs André Daguin, Paul Bocuse, Pierre Troisgros, Madame Lea of Lyon, Christian Millau and Jean Didier. I agreed on the condition that I could be in disguise, for which they provided a yellow wig that seemed to be made of broom straw and a black lace eye and face mask that looked like a whore's garter belt. Wired for simultaneous translation and pretending to eat and sip wine through the satin and lace mask, I fielded barbs from all, faulting Bocuse especially for never being at his restaurant where the public expected him to be, and suggesting that he, like the Queen of England, fly a flag when he is in residence.

As a result, when the three-hour show ended, he grabbed at my mask, trying to pull it off, and after a second attempt, I pushed him, causing him to stumble over an electrical outlet box on the floor. My only regret was that the tussle had not happened while we were on camera.

All of this appealed to the editors of *People* magazine so much that they ran a two-page story, "Who's killing the great chefs of France? Mimi Sheraton proves they dish it out but can't take it."

One small detail indicated just how tight French critics were with the subjects of their reviews. Two of my French friends were in the audience watching the pre-program arrangements and heard Christian Millau say to the chefs, "Let us not *tutoyer* each other, or it will look as though we are friends." (*Tutoyer* refers to *tu,* the familiar form of *you,* used among families and close friends instead of the formal *vous.*)

What could happen when a critic is known became evident a year later when, while visiting the rest of the three stars, we had lunch with two friends at Lameloise, a charming provincial inn in the Burgundy town of Chagny. Our absolutely perfect meal included local classics such as *oeufs pochés en meurette* (poached eggs in a bacon- and shallot-flavored red wine sauce), benchmark escargots sizzling in garlic-parsley butter and a whiff of the region's famed brandy, marc, plus a succulent, gamy pigeon poached *en vessie*—in a pig's bladder—served over foie gras–flecked noodles. All that and 24-karat service led up to the unwanted surprise of being told there was no check. It seemed unlikely that we were having a landmark meal—say the ten-thousandth—and so were being honored. So we insisted on a check, realizing I must have been made. When none was forthcoming, we assured the manager that we would not leave the restaurant until we paid. Finally we got the bill with a 30 percent press discount, but between us scraped together the full amount in cash (lest they destroy a credit card slip), piling it in a heap, center table.

Several years later I heard from a young American chef who had been doing a *stage* in the Lameloise kitchen when I was there, saying he had prepared some of the food I liked. I asked if they knew I was there and if that was why we had to fight for a check. He said that although they did not know just who it was, they knew it was a journalist from the *New York Times*. Then I recalled having asked a secretary in the Paris bureau to confirm my reservation, warning her not to divulge my name or mission. But according to my informant, she had begun the call with "This is the *New York Times* . . ." And so it was.

Operation Otto

OF ALL THE REACTIONS to my work—irate letters to editors, costly full-page advertisements in the *Times* from restaurateurs protesting negative reviews, a few lawsuits and even the juvenile antics of the French—none surprised me more than the ruckus raised over the story my editors and I considered a scoop. Not so the rest of the country's press, including many local newspapers and talk shows, as well as the *Nation*, the *Village Voice*, *Time* and *Newsweek*, most of which excoriated me for uncovering and divulging another writer's secret, and, even more, for ruining the lives of the subjects, or so it was thought. As amusing as I found the entire matter, it did raise the question of standards relating to what a critic or journalist owes both to the reader and to the subject of a story.

My involvement began with a deceptively casual nudge sent on Wednesday, February 15, 1979, to me and Frank Prial, the eloquent wine writer who sometimes also reviewed New Jersey restaurants.

"I hope you both are out there looking for Otto!"

The note was written by Allan M. Siegal, then the news editor of the *New York Times,* and now the assistant managing editor in charge of maintaining journalistic standards. "Maybe it wasn't my business, but I always tend to stick my nose into whatever looks entertaining," Siegal recalled recently. Then, as now, no one took his suggestions lightly, anxious to avoid the more acerbic side of this brilliant and humorous editor's personality.

In the restaurant-obsessed climate of New York during the week of February 12 to 19, 1979, the hottest topic of conversation and conjecture was Otto, the pseudonym of a chef celebrated in the most elaborate terms by John McPhee in the *New Yorker.* In twenty-five thousand well-chosen words, he lauded his subject as the creator of the twenty or thirty best meals the writer had ever had in his life, including even those in "the starry citadels of rural and metropolitan France." Shrinking violets that Otto and his wife were said to be ("he would savor recognition if he could have it without publicity"), they agreed to cooperate with McPhee on a story only on the condition that they, their restaurant and its exact or inexact whereabouts not be named, extracting the promise not to identify even the state or describe the landscape. Hence, "Otto" for the chef and "Anne" for the wife (a member of "one of the First Families of Latvia"), who made the desserts and managed the dining room. Hence, too, the furious competition among restaurant groupies to be the first to find this flawlessly sublime gastronomic hideaway as soon as possible.

What particularly flung the gauntlet and kept the telephones of

food writers, chefs, publicists and restaurateurs ringing off the
hooks were the taunting clues that the skillful McPhee scattered
through the piece. They were completely unnecessary to the tale
except as lures that practically dared readers to discover the mystery subject. We learned that the restaurant's nearest post office
was "more than five miles and less than a hundred from the triangle
formed by La Grenouille, Lutèce and Le Cygne," then New York's
top French restaurants. Farther along, we were teased with details
of the dining room, its "offhand rural European character,"
enhanced by a pair of bullfight prints, two mounted taxidermal
heads, one of a bull and the other of a red fox, Spanish swords,
heavy red curtains, a red tile floor and photographs of what were
called Alaskan dog foxes. "How many such places could there be?"
the food world wondered. "But where?"

In what read like a parody of every a-wonderful-day-in-the-
life-of-a-wonderful-chef article that I had ever read, McPhee
temptingly chronicled Otto's kitchen work, including even his
children's school lunches, his indefatigable shopping trips for haute
and humble ingredients and several critical tours of Manhattan
restaurants. Throughout, he quoted Otto's sincere opinion of his
own talents ("My quenelles are much better than any quenelles you
can actually get anywhere . . .") and of his taste for fast foods such
as McDonald's breakfast sandwich, Egg McMuffin. ("It's a triumph. It's inspired. With melted cheese instead of hollandaise, it is
eggs Benedict for the masses. I don't know why it wasn't thought
of long ago.") McPhee also quoted Otto's judgments of food in
some of New York's loftiest meccas of gastronomy, some of which
he "guessed" were serving frozen ingredients, most especially the
turbot and Dover sole at Lutèce and, at La Caravelle, meat in
which he claimed to have found ice crystals. In an uncharacteristic
lapse of journalistic practice, the *New Yorker*'s legendary fact-

checkers were waved away from this story in deference to McPhee, according to the editor, William Shawn, and so the restaurateurs had no chance to refute the claims before the article appeared. After the piece appeared, they refuted them a lot as did a vast chorus of their fans.

Craig Claiborne, Frank and I seemed to be the only members of the food world who thought the whole matter absurd and overblown, although Frank did conjecture that because McPhee lived in Princeton, Otto must be within driving distance for dinner. The chef's masterpieces did not sound so hot to us, and we felt that McPhee was naïve about his subject's criticisms of other restaurants, offering them without rebuttal. Imagine my surprise that on the very next evening, a frigid and sleet-slicked February night, I found myself in a car with Frank and his wife, Jean, skidding toward the foothills of the Poconos, all in search of the elusive chef.

To find Otto was to get the culinary scoop not only of the week but perhaps the year. I have to admit I just got lucky. Not knowing where to begin, I did nothing when I received Siegal's note, hoping someone else would make the discovery and save me the bother. On Friday, I planned to stay home preparing for a weekend visit from my brother and sister-in-law arriving from Chicago. But early that morning, I received a call from a friend telling me of an article by food editor William Rice in the *Washington Post,* reporting on a conversation he'd had about the likely whereabouts of Otto with Jacob Rosenthal, a former president of the Culinary Institute of America, who kept tabs on chefs and restaurants and who named two possibilities—one being the Red Fox Inn in Milford, Pennsylvania, and another with a name that I have forgotten.

I bought a copy of the *Post,* and began with a telephone call to the Red Fox Inn and was stunned when told that, yes, this was the restaurant that McPhee wrote about. But before I could congratulate

myself, the speaker said he was the new owner and that Otto had
opened another restaurant, the name and location of which would
not be divulged, nor would the chef's real name.

Stumped, I called Frank, who, being an old newspaper hand,
knew just what to do. He simply called the *Times*'s stringer in the
area and directed him to go to the town and find a local politician,
who surely would have dined at all the best spots and know the
whereabouts of restaurateurs. Sure enough, about two hours later
Frank called, telling me to meet him at the office, where we would
get into his car, drive through New Jersey to pick up Jean and pro-
ceed to Shohola, Pennsylvania, where we would dine on the food
of one Alan Lieb at his new Bullhead Inn. (My husband stayed
home to welcome our guests.) Although I mistakenly reported the
town to be Shohola, as did other publications, it was technically in
Twin Lakes, according to Mrs. Lieb, whose first name turned out to
be Anna although she was known by the nickname Ronnie.

By the time we arrived the Liebs knew their secret was out,
probably because the proprietor of the Red Fox had told them of
my call, during which I had identified myself as a reporter for the
Times. Frank, true to his Irish roots, made reservations as Mr.
McCarthy and everyone played it straight including the Liebs, who
gave us a friendly greeting in their rustic restaurant that suggested
a cross between a roadhouse and a ski lodge. We found a few of the
appetizers and main courses to be mildly pleasant if amateurish,
but far short of the excellence McPhee had touted, with only two
cakes, baked by Mrs. Lieb, achieving top rating. Disasters included
dank, musty-tasting snails on brine-soaked artichoke bottoms and
a main course of veal rolls stuffed with clumps of wet bread and
what seemed like raw fatty bacon that Mrs. Lieb later claimed was
prosciutto.

Midway through the meal, we were told there was a phone call
from a Mr. Richards (one of Dick's standard pseudonyms) for any-

one in the McCarthy party. I took it and learned that McPhee had phoned to dissuade me from reviewing the restaurant and from exposing it. Dick told him that I was already there and would not be home until quite late. McPhee asked that I call him whenever I got home, no matter the hour.

After finishing our meal, the three of us practically skated across the icy parking lot to the car, where Frank and I discussed our thoughts. Out on the highway about twenty minutes later, he stopped at a pay phone and called the first story into the *Times* so that it would appear on Saturday morning. I would write a detailed critique on Sunday for Monday's edition.

I returned home at about four A.M. and immediately phoned McPhee. He pleaded for the story to be killed, declaring me, the *Times* and Abe Rosenthal guilty of sensationalism and caring only about selling newspapers. He insisted that he never thought so simple a story about a chef would inspire such fervor. Finally, he accused me of a breach of trust.

"It's not my breach," I said. "I never promised Lieb or anyone else anything and you should not have, either, if you were going to write about him in the *New Yorker*. Anyway, the story is already in and the paper will be dropped on my doorstep in an hour or two. You made this a matter of public interest, especially when food is such a hot topic."

Half musing to himself, McPhee said that perhaps if he had done the same sort of article about a dedicated worker who happened to be a cab driver, the public would not have rushed to find him.

On Monday, my review (without a star rating) appeared in the *Times*. I summed up my opinion of Lieb as someone who was thoroughly sincere and well intentioned, using many fine ingredients but in need of a more developed palate and a better mastery of basic cooking techniques.

In a telephone interview the next day, I asked Lieb if he had

indeed realized we were there and he said yes. He added that he
knew when the McPhee article was published he would have to take
some heat but thought it would be worth it. He apologized to
Lutèce, saying he loved the restaurant but just had never seen fresh
turbot in the Fulton Fish Market and so *guessed* that it was frozen.
Asked if he would again move to escape the Bullhead publicity, he
said only if they were mobbed and overwhelmed. Later Mrs. Lieb
was quoted as saying she was pleased that I had not liked the food
because they would then not be crowded.

Two weeks later, in the March 12, 1979, issue of *Time*, I was
accused of devouring a small inn, being a remorseless critic and operating with the fury of a restaurant critic scorned, while McPhee was
praised for, among other virtues, being a gentleman. In the unsigned
article, the summation was that although the Bullhead Inn might not
be in the class of Michelin three stars, it was "a warm and welcoming
restaurant that draws regular patrons from great distances."

In the same week, *Newsweek* accused me of rarely venturing out
of the city and then gave me more credit than I deserved by
announcing that I had "craftily" phoned a supply company mentioned in the McPhee article as a source for Otto, and thereby got
the restaurant name and address. They also quoted William
Shawn: "It's regrettable that other people couldn't respect this
man's wishes for anonymity . . . It's as if we tried to track down
Thomas Pynchon."

Most vituperative, perhaps, was the entry of the *Village Voice*,
billboarding the story on the front page: "Mimi Sheraton's Bad
Taste," and putting two writers—a reporter and a food critic—on
my case. The first, Geoffrey Stokes, allowed that although I was a
woman of forthright judgment, I was somewhat short on charity,
adding that I wrote this piece with zest. (That was partly true
although my glee was in the joy of discovery.) Acknowledging that
McPhee might have had a "tin palate" and indeed could be wrong

about the food, Stokes judged that the Bullhead Inn would be a very pleasant option for him if it were in his neighborhood.

Then he speculated on the possibility that I had carried a contract, claiming that in the past I had "zapped" the competitors of my cronies, but allowing that the Lieb "attack" seemed to be of no benefit to such acquaintances. He quoted Raymond Sokolov, then the restaurant critic for *Cue* magazine, who conjectured that I, as a New Yorker, decried the food judgment of anyone who, like McPhee, was content to live in Princeton.

In an accompanying *Voice* piece, Joel Oppenheimer, apparently a restaurant critic, said he felt it his duty to report on the Bullhead Inn and then described a thoroughly delightful experience, for the most part including the food.

The notion of a contract also occurred to the writer of a column in the *Nation* (March 24, 1979). Although I was described as being superb and redoubtable, it was suggested that I quite possibly carried a contract on behalf of the *Times*, posing, in classic innuendo, "Or, perhaps, did it have something to do with the rather critical (to management) articles on the New York newspaper strike that ran in the *New Yorker*? The answer to that mystery we shall probably never know."

The only anti-McPhee article appeared in the *New York Post* of March 9 in the lively gossip column that is Page Six. McPhee's "grudging" correction about the fish at Lutèce in the *New Yorker* was repeated by his stating that as far as he was concerned, "the *mea culpa* is strictly Otto's *culpa*."

"Otto guessed wrong," said McPhee, to which the *Post*'s Claudia Cohen added that McPhee forgot to mention that he guessed wrong about Otto. Although I was faulted in several articles for not including "guessed" in describing Lieb's opinion of Lutèce's fish, McPhee, by leaving that estimation unsubstantiated or unquestioned, tacitly implied he thought the chef was right.

If Otto-Alan and Anne-Ronnie felt destroyed by the limelight, they had a funny way of showing it. Some months later they cooperated with *Food & Wine* magazine in a story, complete with Lieb's photograph and recipes from his kitchen, which was among other stories that appeared about him later.

One year and three months after my article appeared, I received an emotional letter from Mrs. Lieb dated May 20, 1980. She had read that I said no review of mine had ever closed a restaurant but she wanted me to know that I had caused the closing of hers. She accused me of destroying a way of life, disrupting her dreams and breaking long relationships among the Liebs and their family of patrons. She insisted that she and her husband had really believed they could remain anonymous despite McPhee's prose, "because very few people read the *New Yorker*."

My answer cited the *Food & Wine* piece as evidence that she and her husband were not quite so shy of publicity as they contended and also explained, "It is our job on this newspaper to respond to public interest, which we did and would do again."

As I think back on Operation Otto, several unanswered questions remain. Had the savvy McPhee deliberately misled the Liebs about the influence of the *New Yorker* for the sake of what he knew would be a great story? Did it ever occur to my various critics that by writing favorable judgments of Lieb's food they might do more to bring on the unwanted crowds than my negative evaluations? Did Alan Lieb, a serious and dedicated chef, secretly crave recognition even with attendant publicity despite his shy wife's reluctance?

The biggest question, perhaps, is whether McPhee knew the difference between what Otto's defenders considered a pleasantly comfortable, homey restaurant with decent, satisfying food that we all value in our own neighborhoods, and a seriously great one, which, in Guide Michelin parlance, is well worth a journey. By posing Otto's restaurant as the latter, he raised expectations that were unfulfilled.

By way of epilogue, many years later, while spending a weekend with friends in the Poconos, I dined unwittingly and, I believe, unrecognized at the third restaurant operated by the Liebs and also named for an animal—first a fox, then a bull, next a dog. But I'm not going to write about that because it is no longer of public interest.

What Makes a Restaurant Tick?

> We are all just soup merchants.
> —*André Soltner*

> People don't come to our restaurants because they're hungry.
> —*Joseph H. Baum*

A S AN UNABASHED LOVER of the entire restaurant phenomenon, I feel that the most magical time of day is thirty to forty-five minutes before the noon lunch opening, a discovery I made as a research consultant to New York's Four Seasons restaurant when it was being created. Even now, I find it exciting to stand on the balcony overlooking the Grill Room at about 11:20 A.M. The scene below suggests a stage set just as the curtain rises with all in readiness for the actors to walk on and the drama to unfold. The white-gold midday sun casts cathedral shafts of light through the copper chain swag curtains, and with its leafy plants, mellow wood paneling and neat patterns of precisely set tables, the room looks orderly and soigné. Yet the atmosphere bristles with a feeling of expectancy that is almost palpable: to paraphrase Nathaniel Hawthorne, I hear the airy footsteps of the strange things about to happen.

By 11:40, the staff drifts into the dining room after a kitchen lunch that forestalls hunger and crankiness during the midday service, just as a five P.M. meal will do before dinner. When I was a consultant, I often felt a flicker of envy if I missed that lunch, as such meals were among the simplest and most delicious the kitchen turned out, unlike the slops reportedly fed to staffs in lesser places. During the early days at the Four Seasons when Albert Stöckli was the chef, I connived to be there on Fridays, when the creamy, garlic-scented fish soup, bourride, was served.

From my perch I watch waiters and busboys glide silently onto the set, adjusting a napkin here, a glass there. Captains double-check the tables in their stations to be sure all are tip-worthy. The maître d'hôtel scans the reservation book to see if high-rolling regulars are seated where they expect to be, hopefully not in embarrassing juxtapositions. Phone calls are made to those who have not yet confirmed their standing reservations so second tier diners-in-waiting will get lucky.

Between 11:50 and 12:15 a few early arrivals place themselves strategically at tables. Some want to see and be seen, others only to see discreetly. The canniest business diners select seats that afford them the most flattering light, and case the menu, deciding what to order so their minds will be free to best unsuspecting counterparts at the art of the deal. Joseph H. Baum, the vice president of Restaurant Associates and the impresario behind that company's most innovative restaurants, liked to recall his days as manager of the bygone Monte Carlo on Madison Avenue and 54th Street, when Ben Sonnenberg came to lunch. The famed publicist would arrive before his guest, satisfy his appetite with something simple, then order only a small salad while recommending a complicated dish like bouillabaise that required difficult, awkward maneuvering, giving Sonnenberg an unencumbered advantage to negotiate.

By the time I became a consultant to the Four Seasons in the winter of 1959, I already had developed sea legs as the food critic for *Cue* and the *Village Voice* and had a sense—at least superficially—of what it was all about. Having given up reviewing when my son was born, I was pleased when Philip Miles, the street-smart publicist for Restaurant Associates, asked me to talk to Joe Baum about doing menu research for the new restaurant-in-progress. I agreed somewhat hesitantly, knowing that Baum had a volatile temper and also feeling conflicted about consulting when I hoped one day to again be a critic. Still, I was tempted because the assignment allowed a flexible work schedule and a generous fee, and I realized that it would initiate me into the behind-the-scenes workings of restaurants.

Most of all, it sounded interesting. Restaurant Associates, with Jerome Brody as president, Joe Baum as the mad but generous genius of a vice president, and a number of other savvy and funny executives already had innovated with successful theme restaurant creations. These included the Newarker, which RA incredibly enough had turned into a special occasion venue in the Newark Airport, the Hawaiian Room in the Hotel Lexington, for which Baum and his executive chef, the Swiss-born Albert Stöckli, invented an entire Chinese-Polynesian cuisine, and the Forum of the Twelve Caesars in Rockefeller Center, a luxurious restaurant with truly excellent food that would rightly be labeled fusion today, drawing as it did upon the history and geography of the Roman Empire.

Unfortunately, the ridiculously overplayed theme (grandiose portraits of the twelve Caesars, silver gladiator helmets as wine buckets, bronze dolphin water taps in the restrooms and brass and bronze service plates embossed with the head of Bacchus, which became the prime targets of pilfering customers) kept the food from being taken seriously. Dishes I still remember with longing include the herb-scented chicken baked in clay that was cracked open most fragrantly at the table, the lobster Jupiter sumptuously poached in a white wine broth, a salad dubbed the Noblest Caesar of Them All, and fiddler crab à la Nero that was among the many dishes flambéed with such exuberant pyrotechnics I feared the whole room might combust. Still, the RA themes offered total theatrical experiences and spiced Baum's menus, as he knew that his audience hungered for more than food.

My first glimpse of the Four Seasons under construction was in sharp contrast to the monumental elegance it achieved and has maintained with a few practical modifications through the regimes of Paul Kovi and Tom Margittai and now under the skillful guidance of Alex von Bidder and Julian Niccolini. What I saw was a dusty, dusky cavern of gray concrete hung with a jungle of biaxial cable as Joe Baum guided me through the obstacle course of drop cloths, pipes, wires, scaffolding and electric outlet boxes. He said the Four Seasons would be the first truly modern American restaurant, reflecting New York's position as the crossroads of the world. The menu would be inspired by dishes from all over the globe with ingredients and cooking techniques freely mixed. In another example of his prescience about Japanese culinary influences and fusion cuisine in general, Baum's menu listed many dishes that would be considered cutting edge today, even in California. Among such were french fried shrimp in shoyu (soy sauce), barquette of flounder with glazed fruits, julep of crabmeat in sweet pepper, herbed lobster parfait, Amish ham steak with a citrus glaze of calamondin fruit and Japanese accents such as wasabi horseradish and soy sauce in Continental and American dishes. Determined to reflect the natural and the seasonal, Baum ordered potted herbs to be grown in the restaurant kitchen and contracted with the composer John Cage, an amateur forager who supplied the restaurant with wild mushrooms from Rockland County, an hour north of Manhattan. Baum's big disappointment was his failure to arrange a permanent supply of organic vegetables from Malabar Farm, the ecological agricultural experiment developed in Ohio by the novelist Louis Bromfield.

My assignment seemed intoxicating. I was to scour through books, magazines, museums and anything else I could think of in search of seasonal food expressions and the customs and recipes surrounding them. When I told my mother about my new assignment she instantly offered advice: "So, you tell them! In summer people want salads, cold soups, corn, watermelon, fresh fruit, things that are light. Winter is the time for your hot soups, stews and pot roasts. What else is there to know?"

Fortunately, I was able to stretch those fundamental truths considerably, else the consultation might have been the shortest on record. (Indeed, it lasted for several years, as I worked on later RA projects.) At a time when even so-called gourmet markets in New York offered champignons as the only mushrooms and iceberg, romaine, Boston, endive and bibb as the only lettuces, I searched for sources of radicchio, mâche, mesclun, fiddlehead ferns, ramps, white asparagus, pomegranates, new almonds in their green suedelike husks, wild mushrooms, fresh truffles and cardoons. I also collected ethnic food lore: rice-harvest festivals in Indonesia, the eating of bitter greens in springtime in the Pennsylvania Dutch country and along the shores of the Adriatic in Apulia, and chervil soup in Germany on Holy (or Green) Thursday, and the good fortune promised by the eating of beans, carp and wheat grains to mark the New Year in many parts of the world. In addition, we gathered a food library to back up Baum's creation, something he always insisted on for his inventions, and sought out highly specialized cooking utensils such as the then virtually unknown Portuguese *cataplana* used for the traditional clam and sausage dish named for that hinged, rounded pot, and the small wooden steamer in which the Japanese prepare the risotto-like rice dish *kamameshi*.

As usually happens, no one learned so much during such a project as the researcher. It proved to be a crash course in international cookery, especially as I was able to hang out in the kitchen and also to sit around listening to all sorts of plans that did not concern me but which I absorbed, especially those that involved James Beard, already a culinary legend and a co-consultant on the project. And I still rely on many cooking tips I picked up from Stöckli: clarifying broth may be a refinement but with each clarification some flavor is lost; a little rice is the best ingredient to bind the sauce for red cabbage, as it also imparts sheen; to avoid soggy boiled potatoes, return them to the empty pot after they are peeled and shake gently over low heat until they look floury.

What I later understood was that the same framework underlying the planning of the Four Seasons applies to restaurants of every class, right down to the corner diner. To prove this to myself, in 1984 I realized one of my dream articles for the short-lived magazine *Manhattan, Inc.* It was an interview with both André Soltner, the four-star chef who made Lutèce perhaps the most outstanding French restaurant this country has had, and the late Leo Steiner, the colorful, street-smart guiding hand behind the Carnegie Delicatessen. Each had lunch in the other's restaurant and viewed the kitchens while discussing the problems of running a restaurant in New York. The biggest difference was in their solutions but, oddly, both found Vulcan ranges to be the best and both thought Dominican workers were the most adaptable of the minorities for kitchen work. Soltner was stunned only by the Carnegie's twenty-two-hour-a-day schedule.

"Who comes here at six o'clock in the morning?" he asked.

"Hookers, show business people, conventioneers, people who work all night and those who start early and need breakfast," Steiner replied.

Two months before the "soft" or unannounced opening of the Four Seasons, we began daily tastings in a banquet room at the Hotel Lexington at which eight or ten of us would sample the creations of Stöckli and the ethereal desserts of Albert Kumin, later to become the White House pastry chef to the Carters. Each day we tasted about thirty-five dishes divided into courses, made our notes and suggested which one should be dropped or retested. No matter how impractical a recipe seemed, it was prepared and sampled if it sounded intriguing, most notably a whole calf's liver braised in Burgundy wine that remains one of the best things I have ever eaten.

"Let's see that again tomorrow," Baum bellowed out to Stöckli, "but with sage instead of thyme."

We also worked out the garnishes and tableside service presentations such as carving of meats and poultry, filleting fish and flambéing crepes, under the direction of Jacques Casanova, a native of Monte Carlo who was the suavest maître d'hôtel New York has ever seen. Only then did we stagger out into the glaring June sunlight of late afternoon, dazed by the food and wine we had sampled in four hours.

I doubt that any restaurant not put together by Joe Baum ever engendered so much painstaking attention to detail. It took two weeks just to decide on the kind of peppercorns for the table and another week to settle on the grind, and almost a month to perfect candied strawberries that cost me the bridgework that I swallowed when the glaze was too sticky. Meanwhile, even more attention was being paid to the decor of the dining rooms by architect Philip Johnson and decorator William Pahlmann. The architecture critic Ada Louise Huxtable and her husband, Garth, designed much of the tableware, which wound up in the collection of the Museum of Modern Art, and Richard Lippold did a Michelangelo for months on scaffolds, hanging the four thousand brass rods of his ceiling sculpture one by one, from two wires each, over the bar and grill areas.

Two weeks before the official opening, there were daily dry runs in the restaurant itself, during which we all had to come for lunch and dinner with friends. We were to order from all over the menu to put the kitchen through its paces, which often became discouragingly slow, as Baum eyed and corrected every dish before it left the kitchen. Walking through the dining room one evening, he asked me what I ordered.

"Goat," I answered.

"You must be crazy, eating goat," he said.

"Then why is it on the menu?"

"Because people are willing to pay more for steak in a place where they could have had goat," he answered, teaching me a lesson in menu psychology.

What I also was learning gradually was the importance of details in creating a restaurant. Knowing how one is put together helped me dissect and evaluate details later as a critic. Everything one sees or uses in a restaurant represents management's choice, even if the choice is not to choose but to let a contractor bring in standard catalogue furniture and tableware. For months, the Four Seasons team debated the height and comfort of the chairs by Mies van der Rohe (the architect who also designed the Seagram Building, where the restaurant was located), but, alas, not the practicality of the blond horsehair upholstery originally on those chairs, although not for long. We tested the workability of knives for cutting steak, the angle of the rims of plates (something rarely done now, judging by the deep soup plates in which many main courses are presented without a thought to the awkwardness of cutting foods in them) and whether lighting created by the masterful Richard Kelly was not only adequate but felicitous and atmospheric.

I began to realize how a restaurateur raises expectations by making promises about goals. That may not be the most important criteria in rating a restaurant, but it does matter to me how close the management comes to delivering on promises made in many ways even before the food is served, beginning with the pre-opening hype—the publicity that touts the background of the chef or owner, the particular cuisine and the elaborate or ingenious decor. Sometimes it's in a name, especially if it's French. One might expect more elegance and finesse from a place that bills itself as Escoffier, Carême or Les Trois Etoiles than from Le Petit Bistro, Joe's or Tony's or the Rib Cage. Descriptions that used to denote a certain class and style of eating place—restaurant, bistro, café, grill, brasserie, trattoria, taverna, osteria—have now blurred beyond meaning as they are interchanged indiscriminately when one or another term becomes fashionable. If bistros or trattorias are in vogue, so be it, whether the food is simple and traditional and is served quickly as the names imply, or is as high-toned and complicated as a Michelin three-star.

Location means a little less now than it used to, especially to dedicated restaurant buffs who are as comfortable with esoteric fare on the Lower East Side as on the Upper East or West Side and anywhere in between. Indeed, in cities everywhere there is a reverse cachet about dining in once seamy, gentrified neighborhoods that in themselves are invitations to those in a downtown state of mind. Still, if a full-fledged restaurant opens in one of our gold coast regions, diners expect it to be toney and expensive and, perhaps, even good.

One of the most telling features of the promise obviously is the restaurant's decor, signaling whether the tone is elegant reserve or boisterous bonhomie, and if the mood and food will be classically traditional, experimentally modern or postmodern fusion and if one is expected to linger or rush in and out. To achieve the last effect, designers use chairs that are not too luxuriously comfortable, as the architect Adam Tihany pointed out to me over lunch in Artisanal as we sat in the small cane chairs similar to those in Parisian sidewalk cafés. (That is also why luncheonette counters rarely have shelves or hooks to comfortably hold customers' handbags or packages, and also why soup and coffee are so often less than steaming hot.) The decor can also define a theme, ethnic or otherwise, and at least hint at the prices. I can think of no better example of how interior design makes a promise and defines an audience than by comparing two fairly recent additions to the New York restaurant scene: Ruby Foo's on Upper Broadway and 66 in TriBeCa. Both are what might be called quasi-Chinese, featuring riffs on that cuisine with overtones of other Asian kitchens. Ruby Foo's, named for a once-famous New York and Boston Chinese predecessor, was designed by the architect David Rockwell. He favors over-the-top theatrical settings such as those he created for the Mohegan Sun casino in Connecticut, the Kodak Theatre in Hollywood, where the Oscar awards are staged, and the soaring multilevel Noche restaurant in Times Square, which like many of his other projects could be the setting for a musical comedy, here Latino, while at Ruby Foo's with its lavish use of lacquer reds and blacks and the abundance of Chinese kitsch might suggest the backdrop for *The World of Susie Wong*. Huge, hectic, crowded and moderately priced, with larger-than-life food presentations that echo the decor, Ruby Foo's appeals to families, large groups and young swingers on the Upper West Side, with its Times Square clone geared mainly to tourists. One look and guests immediately feel as though they are at one big house party.

Starting with its enigmatic name, 66, in the more bohemian environs of TriBeCa, offers no clue as to what it is about nor does a first glance at the spare, coolly white, Bauhaus-informed decor. The only hint is the line of red banners with black Chinese characters hanging over the long, suave counter meant for single diners, those in a hurry or those who like to talk to strangers. Designed by Richard Meier as his first, and, he claims, his only restaurant, 66 reflects his taste for classic modern architecture that has distinguished his buildings such as the High Museum in Atlanta and the Getty Center in Los Angeles and many others in Europe and the States. A man who likes any color as long as it's white, Meier here created a restrained, shimmering interior with honey-colored bamboo floors and furniture by Charles Eames and Eero Saarinen; he divided spaces with high-tech steel grid panels that somehow suggest Japanese shoji screens. With high prices and neatly adequate but never opulent portions, 66 draws designers, artists and celebrities of all sorts with a taste for esoteric chinoiserie—some of the staff dresses in Mao jackets and Cantonese and Sichuan favorites are modified by French, Thai and Japanese accents.

All three designers said their work begins with the style of the food, not often clearly articulated by the chef, and so they see and taste it for themselves, then try to match the spirit of the cuisine in the setting. Unless a restaurant is in a space built to order from scratch, they must work between two fixed points—the main entrance door and the kitchen. Adam Tihany explained that when designing an elegant restaurant he likes to plan a separate foyer entrance that hints at the splendor to come, while at a convivial, informal brasserie like Artisanal, guests are immediately plunged into the action. Among unexpected errors he has since corrected is the position of the restaurant's checkroom.

"First we had it in the back of the restaurant, but women were unhappy about handing fur coats over without seeing where they were hung. So we moved it up front."

Other logistical problems designers face is getting customers, especially New Yorkers, to go to upstairs or downstairs dining rooms, something they solve with carefully planned staircases or elevators, especially enticing decors and, I often suspect, even shills to make those areas look desirably crowded.

I learned the full importance of making promises in menus when I participated in the writing of them for the Four Seasons. Diners may peruse menus for their pleasure, but few realize just how critical a document a menu can be and how many functions it performs for the management. By the graphics, paper and language the menu announces the level of quality and sophistication the management claims for itself. That is only a little less true today, as computer printers allow for some elegant and elaborate designs that can be changed daily and reproduced inexpensively. Printed on vellum in the old days of typesetting, and covered with silk-threaded Japanese rice paper, the original Four Seasons menu was so expensive that before adding a dish, Baum, Stöckli, and their purchasers made very sure of the steady availability of an ingredient and the stability of its price. When one consultant assured Baum that morels would be available for a certain seasonal dish, he warned, "If I print them on this menu, you better find them even if you have to grow them in your armpits." Ever since, I have felt funny about ordering those spongy, earth-dark and deliciously smoky wild mushrooms, wondering where indeed they might have been cultivated.

At its most basic, the menu is an offer to sell, listing choices and prices, except for a few dated outposts where, ridiculously if not insultingly, no prices appear on menus for guests or women. The language tells much as well, from the simplest descriptions on coffee shop or steak house menus to the ultimate pretension, saying it in a foreign language—usually French—without translation. Of all the menu sins that may be committed, none bothers me more than obfuscation, not giving the diner a clue as to what sort of dish to expect. In that respect, a menu completely in a foreign language is only one type of confusion. Others I have seen include obscure culinary terms without clarifications such as *talmouse* (a triangular puff pastry traditionally with a cheese filling) or *attereaux* (tiny skewers holding bits of fried meat or seafood). Similarly, the diner should get an idea as to the nature of exotic ingredients such as, for example, ponzu, the citrus-soy sauce patrons might be expected to know only in a Japanese restaurant although it has now gone multinational. Much the same is true of *frico,* the Friulian lacy cheese crisp that even on Italian menus might need explanation to many. In the name of fusion and culinary postmodernism, new menu language often inspires wrong expectations. I can be reasonably sure of what I will get when ordering chicken bouillabaise, but I might get cranky if a dish billed as a warm salad of beef and garden vegetables arrived as beef stew, unexpected soupiness being a frequent surprise these days.

More strategically, a menu is a way of controlling kitchen activity and economics. When well planned, it offers a variety of dishes that distributes the kitchen work among the grill, roasting oven, the range for sautéed or fried foods and the cold station (a.k.a. the *garde manger*) that is responsible for side and main course salads and cold appetizers because it is located in the coolest part of the kitchen. Pre-cooked dishes such as braised meats and stews or roasts take pressure off cooking stations at peak times.

From the management's point of view, the menu serves to balance costs and improve profits. To understand how dishes on menus are priced is to grasp restaurant economics that result in pasta that may cost eighteen or twenty-two dollars, why half portions are not half priced and why many establishments have minimums or only price-fixed complete table d'hôte menus.

Although it is logical to assume that food is what you are buying in a restaurant, that is only about one-third true. What you really are paying for is real estate. You are renting the premises for a given amount of time that expands or contracts with the price level of the restaurant. Spend five hundred dollars for two and you should be able to stay for the entire evening, if not for the entire weekend. Spend twenty-five dollars for two in Chinatown or at a pizzeria and see if they let you sit there for more than an hour, if that long. So critical is the ratio of space to price that most designers work within a formula devised by the American Institute of Architects (AIA) in their book *Architectural Graphic Standards* that charts the square footage to be allotted per person in various classes of restaurants: the least space per customer—10 to 12 square feet—is allowed on banquet premises, while 10 to 16 are standard for a tearoom. A cafeteria should allot 12 to 18 square feet per person, and a lunchroom/coffee shop, 12 to 16. In a restaurant dining room, 13 to 16 square feet is the rule, while the most spacious accommodations, 17 to 22 square feet per person, are granted for specialty/formal dining. That square footage includes the chair and the room to slide it in and out.

A restaurant is essentially a retail operation, and its costs and income are figured on a square foot basis on dining room space only and covers utilities, laundry, flowers or other items of decor, insurance and the rest. Therefore, the nonfood meter ticks away at the same rate whether you order spaghetti and meatballs or breast of guinea hen under glass.

Traditionally the formula for food cost is one-third, meaning that the owner's cost of all ingredients in a dish (without labor) should add up to one-third of the retail or menu price. According to Michael Lomonaco, the very skillful and amiable chef who has held forth deliciously at places such as the '21' Club, La Caravelle, Windows on the World and Noche, a one-third food cost is still mostly correct, but he adds, "The pencil has gotten sharper since costs across the board have risen. Food cost is now best seen as between 28 and 32 percent of food sales, while labor and related costs should be between 30 and 35 percent of total sales, liquor included, operating expenses should range from 12 to 15 percent of total sales, and rent, less than 8 percent of the total."

Such percentages for food represent an average between low-cost and high-cost ingredients. Many restaurants must have certain foods regardless of price. Beef is essential to a steak house or for the pastrami and corned beef necessary in a New York–style delicatessen, just as shellfish is mandatory at seafood houses and in a certain class of restaurants that must have some as appetizers. If the wholesale price of something like truffles, lobster, crabmeat, beef or caviar is very high, the item will not sell at a triple markup and so will spoil. The restaurateur then must take a lower markup, if any, on those items and try to compensate by making less expensive foods such as pasta, potatoes, codfish or chicken more tempting to his diners. This he does by dressing up inexpensive ingredients with enticing garnishes and seasonings (and, often, language) that add to the customers' perception of value. Other opportunities for improving profits are soup, coffee, tea, bottled water and liquor of any kind, none more so than wine by the glass, the price of which, according to the *New York Times*'s Frank Prial is usually the amount the restaurateur paid for the entire bottle that pours four to five portions.

Still another profit-inflating technique, and one that I consider unethical, is the recitation of off-menu "specials" without stating their prices. Such choices almost always cost a good deal more than the highest prices listed on the menu. It is mostly the public that is to blame because very few ask the prices, finding it embarrassing, either as guest or host. Such scams really should be illegal, considering how simple it would be to print out specials with prices, but consumerism at the caviar level will hardly become a populist cause.

Labor costs matter, too, as do the decor and its upkeep. A steak house like the original Palm in New York has a high food cost but relatively low kitchen labor costs in terms of handwork, and lower maintenance than high-style restaurants with elaborately arranged dishes and glamorous accessories. At the beautiful and excellent La Grenouille in Manhattan, the cost of the lavish floral bouquets sets owner Charles Masson back some $140,000 a year, amortized in the pricing of every dish. That explains why an unadorned but perfect one-and-a-half-pound prime sirloin steak at the Palm costs $35.50 while an eight- to ten-ounce filet mignon at La Grenouille is $42. You pays your money and you takes your choice, and often the occasion dictates that choice.

Restaurateurs also sometimes determine price in terms of what the traffic will bear. At the early Four Seasons menu planning sessions, Joe Baum and Jerry Brody referred to a set of menus from restaurants they considered competitive: the '21' Club and the bygone Le Pavillon and the Colony, among others, and so priced against them, trying never to be consistently higher or lower on every dish. In one memorable session, Baum, with a daredevil twinkle in his eye, challenged, "Let's see if we can get a buck for a martini." (Today a martini at the Four Seasons is $15.)

A restaurateur's chances at profitability obviously are much greater with a minimum ten-year lease at a stable rent or, still better, ownership of the building with some rental space, allowing many to ride out dire recessions. Rents are invariably higher if the location delivers an audience, as in the Theater District, Lincoln Center, or atop skyscrapers that afford a view, which is why it is rare to find great food in such locations. A truly talented chef can command a loyal clientele almost anywhere, without paying a premium in rent.

For the standard one-third formula to work, all costs must be in line, in a sense representing a cohesive ambition. As obvious as that may seem, one of the most common errors among restaurateurs is to have the quality level of the food out of whack with the decor and the necessary price. It would be ridiculous, if not fatal, to an establishment to serve takeout Chinese noodle soups in a lavish setting of fragile accessories and costly floral arrangements. The amount customers would be willing to pay for that soup could not cover the maintenance costs or the rent in a prime area. Less obvious perhaps, but also surprisingly common, is the owner whose ego demands a very elegant and expensive establishment but whose chef is not good enough to justify the price. In the end, only a truly talented chef can execute dishes that seem incomparable and, therefore, worth almost any price. Hardest pressed as costs rise are family and neighborhood restaurants with a moderate ambition and dependable performance, which have to charge more than the overall experience seems to be worth.

These days I find myself increasingly resenting prices for nice, satisfying and even slightly stylish meals in local neighborhood restaurants where we go when I don't feel like cooking, and winding up with a check for sixty-five to seventy-five dollars for two courses and one glass of wine each. On the other hand, we rarely resent spending two hundred dollars for dinner if the experience is unique and memorable with food that is at once revelatory and delicious served in felicitous surroundings by a wait staff that is politely and efficiently invisible and never intrusive or cornily overbearing.

Such dream staffs are hard to come by, considering that in many industry surveys the public's main complaint about restaurants is service. Usually blame falls to waiters, but I feel that for the most part, the real crisis is with management that either does not recognize inept service or turns a blind eye to it. It is hard to believe that anyone, including even a part-timer en route to another career, really is happy doing a bad job, given the resultant flak from customers and the lower tips. Too often, guidance and real training are lacking. It is discouragingly common to see a managerial type walking through dining rooms as someone told him to do, without spotting problems or lending a helping hand or offering gentle corrections. I think such a type generally is either the product of a restaurant or hotel management school (much in the style of MBAs who have no real feeling for the particular business they are in) or an owner who envisions himself as an affable mine host.

Dining room staffs often reflect the attitude of bosses toward the clientele. There is a surprisingly large number of very efficient restaurateurs who, like the late, legendary Henri Soulé at Le Pavillon, have contempt for many of their patrons, feeling them somehow unworthy, and who impart that feeling to their staffs. At times, a rave review in an influential magazine or newspaper can make management and staff feel they have it made and need not suffer a particular customer, since so many will be flocking there.

One such example occurred when I gave a three-star rating to a good and authentic, moderately priced bistro. In the true spirit of French frugality, the owner overbooked without adding extra help. Among those who rushed to try it was Abe Rosenthal, who, most unusually, did not identify himself. He was at my desk fuming by 9:30 the morning after, complaining that he was told that even though he had a reservation, he would have to wait for at least forty-five minutes and could not get a drink at the service bar.

"We had a three-star review from the *New York Times*," a frantic manager told him, "so you can leave if you want to."

After a few more similar reports from readers, I included a caveat about the reported service in my next column, not that it discouraged many who hungered for bargains in good bistro fare.

There obviously are varied sources for wait staffs, depending in part on the class of the restaurant. Owners of small, casual eating places in low-rent neighborhoods might merely hang a "Help Wanted" sign in the window or on a nearby college bulletin board and hope to get lucky. Under the most sophisticated circumstances, a restaurateur may hire an experienced manager or maître d' who brings with him waiters and captains he has worked with. Many restaurateurs hold open calls on certain days so candidates can apply. And not to forget, if all else fails, there is always stealing, a well-known practice among owners who shop the competition less for food than for efficient help. First-time restaurateurs lacking a track record rarely attract top waiters who are reluctant to leave high-tipping jobs for an unknown. Often, however, experienced help applies after a favorable review, knowing that at least in the short run, there will be plenty of customers.

In addition to there always being a shortage of the best, a problem with finding good dining room help is that in this country, such jobs impart little social status, now even diminishing as the real action and stardom shifts from the dining room to the kitchen. Today the chef is king and controls the presentation of dishes with plated service. One solution offered by many owners is that tipping be automatic here as in Europe so that waiters do not feel that they are at the mercy of diners. It is a proposal I strongly disagree with, as the tip remains our best defense against poor service.

Good service no longer means what it used to, nor should it. Although efficient, the old-style Swiss hotel school mannerisms seem corny and stuffy today and a new tone is much in order. Joe Baum went a long way to developing that, if sometimes in an exaggerated way, as when at the Tower Suite atop the Time-Life Building he first had waiters introduce themselves with "I am Kevin. I will be your waiter tonight." A casual, egalitarian tone is set without sacrifice of efficiency or respect most notably at New York restaurants such as those owned by Danny Meyer (Union Square Cafe, Gramercy Tavern and Blue Smoke among others), at Drew Nieporent's Tribeca Grill and at the Four Seasons, where the reserved but not subservient tone Joe Baum established still prevails.

My own feeling is that at a minimum the staff should be polite, just as I think a restaurant should first of all be clean. Not everyone can be efficient, but politeness and cleanliness are in the reach of everyone, and it has struck me that the Italian word for clean is *pulito*, hinting, perhaps, at a philosophical connection.

To the much asked question of how I arrive at restaurant ratings, I answer: All of the above. For though I do not carry a checklist, or consciously separate each and every aspect at every moment, I think my experiences with the Four Seasons and later projects for Joe Baum and Jerry Brody have enabled me to take it all in, digest it and arrive at a rating, a process which, Abe Rosenthal once remarked, "seems Talmudic."

The Care and Feeding of Passengers, Patients and Other Captives

DESPITE THE FUN OF REVIEWING RESTAURANTS, that was by no means my only interest, nor the most serious and challenging. Long before I went to the *New York Times,* I developed a somewhat perverse, if not morbid, curiosity about institutional food served to captive audiences. The more captive the audience (as in prisons, or in hospitals and schools that prohibit patients or students from leaving the premises or bringing in food), the less management has to try to please and the greater the customer dissatisfaction *even when the food is good,* a psychological factor well known to food service managers. In catering to a noncaptive audience—one that can choose to eat outside of institutions such as employee, museum and college cafeterias, the management must compete and so tries harder—or should.

Through the years, this interest led me to investigate 150 lunches in public and private schools in New York, New Orleans, Milwaukee, Chicago, Newark, Las Vegas and Kansas City, Kansas, and the results of my research appeared in a two-part front-page story in the *New York Times* in 1976. Ten years later I flew around the world in business class on eleven different airlines to report on meals for *Condé Nast Traveler* at the request of the magazine's innovative and imaginative founding editor, Harry Evans. I have spoken at conventions of hospital and airline food service management and visited about a dozen institutional food trade shows where displays featured the latest futuramic, labor-saving (job-cutting) convenience foods such as canned beef sauce that was described as "institutional strength gravy" and robotic equipment said to be "idiot proof," a claim eventually disproven because the ingenuity of idiots was greatly underestimated. I have toured at least a dozen airline kitchens in various parts of the world and, for the *New York Observer,* I reported on the punitive inmate food at Riker's Island and the almost as punishing fare in several museum cafés. For *Premier* magazine, I sampled the meals of caterers who service film crews on location, and for the short-lived *National Sports Daily,* I reviewed the dismal grub in ballparks around the country. For articles in *Time* I landed in helicopters on two off-shore oil rigs in the Gulf of Mexico (talk about a captive audience) and also traveled throughout China for a month in 1987, where, between ten-course banquets and pyramids of street dumplings, I researched food in hospitals and employee and school cafeterias. My goal always was to find those outposts—if any—that produced decent to excellent food, on the theory that if even one kitchen can do a good job under a given set of conditions, so can all kitchens working under the same conditions.

I had my first taste of institutional food in high school (in my day, elementary school children either went home for lunch or carried lunch boxes) and, later, in employee cafeterias. Gradually, as I flew on airplanes, spent occasional periods in hospitals and traveled on highways where fast-food chains have monopoly contracts with states (motorists reluctant to exit the thruways are self-made captives), I gained generally grim knowledge of the subject, always thinking of how the depressing concoctions served could be improved. What I usually found is all too well known—the wilted vegetables and salads, insipid breads, generic gray meats, the pasty gravies and gummy bottled dressings, too finely pulverized tuna and chicken salads much like wads of wet, matted cloth, soups slippery with cornstarch, and the sweet-sour-salty flavor of convenience anything—all food that is at once totally bland yet nerve-wrackingly offensive.

I often wonder how any food could possibly be so badly prepared and handled. In *noir* moments at hospitals or on long flights, I try to figure out how I would go about re-creating the horrors before me. Where would I start? In what diabolical cookbook would one find such recipes? On what ignominious grocery shelf is the special seasoning marked "Institutional" that is surely used to impart the characteristic flavor and aroma, a combination of chemicals, foodishness, stale sweetness and desolation? I will never forget one airline "snack"—a sticky, warm and sour-smelling ham and cheese sandwich—for which the last line of the recipe must have read, "Hold in your armpit for three hours before serving."

My interest in the problems of institutional food began with a book I found many years ago at a secondhand bookstore. It was a totally bedraggled but much appreciated copy of *Culinary Campaign,* written by Alexis Soyer, the French chef who made his reputation in Victorian London at the private Reform Club. Not resting on his haute cuisine laurels, Soyer wrote books for home cooks on limited budgets. *Culinary Campaign,* published in 1857, recounts Soyer's travels to Scutari (now Üsküdar) on the Asian side of the Bosphorus in Turkey during the Crimean War. He went at the request of the British government to improve meals both in field encampments (for which he eventually invented special stoves and cooking utensils) and in the military hospital where the nursing staff and services were run by Florence Nightingale. With her cooperation and some cooks he had brought with him, Soyer set about redesigning and improving dishes at no additional cost.

Before Soyer's intervention, soup and its boiled beef were served as separate courses, resulting in meat that was dry and cold by the time it was delivered to patients. Soyer's solution, in addition to improving flavor by pre-salting (corning) the beef and adding some fresh root vegetables and herbs, was to cut the beef into spoon-size chunks and serve it right in the soup as a single course, so the meat would stay moist and hot—an exquisitely simple solution of the sort I cherish.

Soyer's efforts came back to me in the very hot July of 1967, when I was a patient in University Hospital of New York University (now the Tisch Hospital). We were renovating our house and an uninstalled radiator fell on my foot, smashing the bone and tearing the skin so badly that I needed a graft. In those days, doctors could hospitalize patients as long as they deemed necessary and because the skin graft required me to keep my foot elevated to prevent swelling, and because we lived on three floors, I stayed for two weeks. I was not in pain and so had time to be bored and, thrice daily, disgusted by the food I complained to my doctor: "I'm fine. It's the food that's sick!" I assured him that it did not have to be so bad. Finally, to shut me up, he brought first the food service manager, Dean Lage, who in turn brought Irving Wilmot, the director of the hospital, to hear me out.

I left the hospital with a one-year contract to improve food for patients as well as for the visitors' coffee shop then in the lobby, all to begin as soon as I could walk. During my two months of convalescence, I studied up on methods of quantity cooking. The most helpful books on the subject were *The Cook Book of the United States Navy*, published by the U.S. Navy Bureau of Supplies and Accounts, and *Cooking and Baking on Shipboard*, the official manual of the War Shipping Administration. Most of the recipes served 100, but a stunner was for 1,000 one-cup portions of Knickerbocker Bean Soup. Just the notion of ladling it out cupful by cupful seemed daunting to me, never mind the preparation. The recipe called for 36 gallons of boiling water, 3½ quarts of cubed salt pork, 24¼ gallons of beef stock, 7⅓ gallons of canned tomatoes and equally staggering amounts of white beans, carrots, onions, potatoes, bacon fat, salt and pepper. What was not stated was the size of the cauldron in which all were cooked, but there was probably not even enough room to slip in thyme, bay leaves and caraway seeds that would have perked up the flavor.

Because recipes give form to function, they are designs in the strictest sense of the word. Following Soyer's example, I hoped to design or adapt dishes that could be satisfactorily prepared within the methods, budget, capabilities and limitations of the gargantuan hospital kitchen with its relatively untrained, diverse staff and a strong union. I envisioned food that would stay hot and survive well en route from basement kitchen to patients on all floors and in several wings. For example, steaks, hamburgers and sliced roast beef without sauce or gravy and kept warm with heat pellets under plates would invariably arrive in the patient's room gray, dry and tough. Braised meats such as pot roasts and stews would hold up far better. Hamburgers or chopped steaks topped with a light tomato sauce would remain moist and flavorful. This assumed, of course, that gravies and sauces would be delicious and light and not the usual floury mass that patients reject or order on the side. Similarly, vegetables needed a protective glossing of a light vegetable oil or butter and a sprinkling of green herbs, especially parsley, so they did not become tasteless and limp. I ruled out anything breaded and fried—less for health reasons than for aesthetics, as breading steams and goes mushy if covered while hot.

As I began to test in smaller quantities for which ingredients—especially liquids—are not always reduced proportionately, I seasoned those institutional recipes as recommended in my favorite cookbooks, by Julia Child, Elizabeth David, Ada Boni *(The Talisman Italian Cookbook),* my own *The German Cookbook* and my personal repertory. When fully ambulatory, I began working with the hospital's chief cook, upgrading specifications for the products we purchased and testing recipes in batches of 100 that were sold in the employee cafeteria.

While working through this routine, I became aware of many of the real-life obstacles that accounted for the well-known slip between the cup and the lip—the wide gap between genuinely good intentions and bad results. At the outset, a hospital is bound to have problems feeding a large population. Patients are ill and frightened and, in an urban situation where there is a wide ethnic mix, each group regards familiar food as a sign of being acknowledged. Yet whenever ethnic fare is presented, it usually is found wanting—not the way Mother made it. Special diets create other problems, both in production and patient satisfaction. Is anyone going to be happy with unsalted food or a soft diet of Cream of Wheat and mashed potatoes? As most hospitals do, this one offered choices on menus, another production problem but worth tackling because it appeases patients. Factor into that the cost of food and labor, and the problems are compounded.

Among other admonitions was one that amused me: I was not to put any organ meats on the menu, lest we offend patients who were being treated for a heart, lung, brain, liver or kidney ailment. I refrained from asking if that prohibition extended to leg of lamb, head lettuce, rump roast, chicken breast and rib-eye steak. Another minor surprise came when I was planning what turned out to be very well-received, salt-free Thanksgiving dishes for special diets. Relying on many herbs and vegetables that would add flavor complexity, I braised a lot of celery with onions and carrots, only to be told that celery was verboten—too high in sodium.

Backed up firmly and amiably by Dean Lage, who was well liked by the kitchen staff, I generally felt no outward hostility to my suggestions. Only occasionally, where a more labor intensive process was recommended, did a few workers complain to the union shop steward, who, to his credit, placated rather than confronted. But even in the best spirit of cooperation, natural differences emerged, especially with seasonings. When I devised a recipe for Italian tomato sauce, Hispanics cooks seasoned to taste—their taste—which meant adding cumin and chili powder. Or a woman who cooked good Caribbean food at home decided that all a dish needed was a hefty shot of hot sauce. Or a Swiss or German cook felt nothing tasted right without browned onions.

Sometimes there were unforseeable misunderstandings. When I experimented with a version of sauerbraten, I demonstrated the skimming off of all grease from the gravy and then went to the cafeteria to see how this was playing out on the line. I looked into the well holding the gravy and saw only an opaque golden shimmer. Yes, they had meticulously skimmed off the grease, but they sent that up with the meat after discarding the real gravy, an error so blatant I wondered, paranoiacally, if it was deliberate.

As months progressed and I watched the kitchen action, the bored and exhausted staff working on assembly lines, trying to get through a day and punching out for the shift, and the vast quantities of ingredients and the size of cooking vessels, I began to realize that there are some basic psychological attitudes about institutional food service that mitigate against its being consistently good.

For one thing, feeding is not the prime purpose of an institution. A hospital is to cure, a school to teach, a prison to punish (if not rehabilitate), an airline to transport and companies to perform services or make products, and, with luck, profits. Most managements, therefore, regard feeding as a necessary evil and a pretty annoying one at that, considering the costs and the justifiable concern with safety. And so when budgets tighten, institutions, understandably, make cuts in food rather than reduce their primary services.

Then there is the natural dissatisfaction on the part of the audience. In any institution there is a distrust of the motives of the management and those in authority, to say nothing of the sheer boredom of having to eat in the same surroundings day after day. Especially in schools, it is considered uncool to have breakfast or lunch in the cafeteria, partly a reaction to nerdishness but also because in our large urban centers so many students qualify for free or partially subsidized lunches that there is a stigma to being seen there.

From the production side of institutional food, there is the impersonal aspect of large-scale preparation and the fact that kitchen workers rarely see the people they cook for, making it very hard to care how it all turns out, cooking being one of the many endeavors for which direct praise—or blame—are the spurs. I also believe that even the best cook can lose respect for food handled in giant vat-size quantities such as those indicated for the 1,000-portion Knickerbocker Bean Soup. Adding salt in pinches suggests a delicate and refined discernment that is not operative when dumping in two or three cupfuls. The German language has two words for eating—*essen,* which is what people do, and *fressen,* which is what animals do. The English counterpart would be to say that people eat food, but animals feed on feed, not food. And feed is what most institutional kitchens turn out.

Given the complexities of cooking and the volume of 7,500 daily meals served at University Hospital, I became less puzzled by bad food than by the fact that any patient managed to get even a cup of hot coffee, never mind a crust of bread. For the record, my work with that hospital realized its greatest success with special diet menus and the profitable coffee shop, now closed because of space limitations. Soberingly enough, my efforts had no lasting effect, as old methods were reverted to as soon as my assignment was completed. Judging by my more recent incarcerations in that hospital, the food has become even worse.

My tour through schools was even more alarming than my hospital duty, because of much more constraining elements—a huge civic bureaucracy burdened with waste and incompetency at all levels, an inadequate budget, shorter time to serve and eat meals and a difficult audience at best. I reported during an especially awful, cautionary period when cooking kitchens in many New York City elementary and intermediate schools were ripped out and replaced by highly specialized (and so highly restrictive) convection ovens that would heat (reconstitute) tiny, individual frozen meal packs—much like miniature TV dinners. Most of this food was vile: thin, gray curling hamburgers much like the soles of old shoes, grilled cheese sandwiches as limp as wet towels, sweaty hot dogs and orangey, grease-laden spaghetti overcooked to a sodden mass. Stuck with no cooking equipment, the Board of Education found itself in thrall to the suppliers of meal packs, illustrating the error of allowing no options. In addition, kids had to negotiate meals using only a spork—a wobbly plasticized paper spoon notched at the tip to suggest a fork. This virtually useless utensil is still in use, as no knives are permitted.

In schools as in other institutions, the big difference in food quality is the one-person-who-cares factor. Such dedication comes even at the public school level, as I discovered in one of the most crowded high schools in Manhattan in 1976. The same restrictions and government-donated food commodities prevailed there as in all other city schools, and I found the food to be far above average—copious, hot, well-seasoned with inviting choices and presentation. The reason was the cook in charge, a man who knew how to prepare food and cared about the kids. At that school came a sobering encounter. Because there were many African-American students, some so-called soul food—southern specialties—were available. Noticing that one tall African-American senior was reaching for pizza and a hamburger, I asked him if he ever chose the tempting collard greens, mashed sweet potatoes and fried chicken. "Nah," he said. "I get that shit at home." This, at a time when ethnic polarization was at one of its peaks in New York City and each group of parents fought, demonstrated and dumped food delivery trucks in the street, demanding that their ethnic foods be offered at school. Meanwhile, all of the children I queried said they wanted "American" food: pizza, spaghetti, meatballs, chili, peanut butter or melted cheese sandwiches, fried chicken, french fries, corn, hamburgers and hot dogs—things that were quick and easy to consume and did not stigmatize kids as being different, a great concern during teen years.

Different parameters in both public or private schools, in New York and other cities, resulted in much better food. In addition to the someone-who-cared factor were lower labor costs that encouraged more cooking from scratch, thereby producing fresher food and, in public schools, making more economical and appealing use of the commodities such as milk, flour, cheese, ground beef, peanut butter, and fruit donated by the U.S. Department of Agriculture as a way of using the surpluses for which farmers received subsidies. Schools that did not do their own cooking sent donated commodities to processors at additional cost and with less control over the final product. In Milwaukee, where the student body then was less diverse and less contentious than in New York, there were no menu choices. All students had the same daily menu for which everything, including hamburger rolls, was made from scratch in each school. To avoid the feeling that the menus are imposed upon them by adults, committees of high school students met regularly with management to decide on menus, new recipes and products. I have no idea if such a system is still followed in Milwaukee, but it resulted in the best school lunches I had during that tour.

Better meals also resulted when the student body was fairly homogeneous and shared the same preferences, a factor made obvious in New Orleans, where labor costs were low and kids liked southern specialties such as red beans and rice, chili, chicken in many forms, and local versions of Italian dishes in addition to the usual favorites. Much the same principle operated in Jewish parochial schools in Brooklyn and Manhattan. Dairy menus were generally the norm (else two kitchens—one for meat, the other for dairy—would be required) and children were used to eating many soups, egg and tuna fish salads, raw vegetables with sour cream, blintzes and, as Middle Eastern–Israeli dishes became known, tabbouleh, hummus and falafel often sandwiched into pita. Also, religious schools usually could supplement their budgets as necessary with contributions from church or synagogue members.

In 2003, the management of the newly created New York City Department of Education initiated a plan to improve school breakfasts and lunches. I volunteered as an adviser but soon resigned, primarily because my tight schedule made meaningful participation impossible but also because I was kept out of much strategic planning when I refused to sign a confidentiality agreement requiring that no one working on the project would discuss any aspect of it without management approval. I still wonder what schemes they anticipated that were diabolical enough to warrant sworn secrecy.

I am also skeptical about the success of this three-to-five-year plan that can be realized only if the same political party holds the office of mayor. So far, the few changes made are not encouraging. Foremost among such is the involvement of Snapple (fruit drinks high in sugar and calories), the company that offered the city $166 million a year to become our "official" beverage made available in school vending machines, among other venues. There are also the announced high-carbohydrate breakfasts combining such offerings as a muffin, a doughnut, fruit juice and cereal on a single tray that were presented as models. Considering the high rate of obesity and diabetes among schoolchildren, some of the plans are already being widely and wisely criticized.

As a final Catch-22, schools face the problem of low participation in breakfast and lunch programs, most of which are geared to needy children whose meals are wholly or partially subsidized by the federal government if they meet approved nutritional standards. In order to operate at no loss (never mind a profit), schools need high volume so the combined subsidies cover their costs. Children I have questioned in elementary and high schools all say they would eat in the cafeteria if the food were better. School food service people feel the food could be better if participation were greater. I doubt both claims.

It is to be hoped, however, that new plans will include brighter lunchrooms. Now, as when I did my original research, cafeterias in most public schools are discouragingly drab. Typical was one I recently visited that had totally blank, stone-gray walls. I asked if some posters and pictures might not brighten things up and was told by the manager that such hangings provide hiding places for cockroaches.

Sadly, most school lunchrooms with their cheerless colors and gated or barred windows are not much more inviting than those I saw on Riker's Island. My story for the *New York Observer* in 1994 was prompted by an announced new plan costing taxpayers $315.4 million to change the method of preparing food in the sixteen prisons operated by the New York City Department of Corrections. The plan was known as cook-chill, a method I had already seen in a hospital and found wanting. Cooking to 160 degrees, then quickly chilling and storing just above the freezing point, gave food a two-day to two-week shelf life. It was then to be reheated to 160 degrees just before being served. Anyone who cares about good food has to question a method that has the staff cooking every day but then serving cold-storage food that is two weeks old.

Far grimmer than the food I eventually tasted was the experience of being in the oldest facility on Riker's Island, the James A. Thomas Center, with a cornerstone laid in 1933 by Mayor James J. Walker. Despite the rather handsome though neglected reception room that is an Art Deco landmark, as I walked through the corridors to the kitchen through the cellblock area, I felt unnerved and somewhat embarrassed as I glimpsed the cells that were stacked cages, suggesting a human zoo or a set for a Beckett play. Old but clean, the kitchen in that center was staffed with prisoners who prepared trays to be given to obstreperous inmates, who had to eat in their cells. I tasted the pizza slices being served in a staff lunchroom and found them limp, sodden and heavily zapped with bitter oregano, salt and pepper, much overseasoned, as most dishes were here due to inmate demand. A salad of iceberg lettuce seemed like cruel and unusual punishment, helped only slightly by fresh tomatoes and cucumbers. Kool-Aid and tea were the beverages although decaffeinated coffee could be requested.

I was taken to the much more modern George A. Vierno Center, where that evening's main course was in preparation. It was chicken orientale, made with fresh chicken pieces, green peppers, onions and carrots and I described it as minimally decent, although it was hard to tell why it qualified as "orientale." My sampling was hardly promising, but hardly conclusive because it represented such a small percentage of the 54,000 meals then prepared on the island, where thirteen daily menus were mandated to satisfy all religious and health-related concerns. The experience raised the question of just how much sympathy one should have for criminals receiving poor to lackluster food and whether the public would be willing to spend more to improve such meals. My own view is that it diminishes one's self to deliberately give poor food to any human being, even if luxurious fare is hardly in order.

By contrast, it was a kick to visit movie sets on different locations, with food prepared by various caterers, and to learn that Clint Eastwood's day is made if he can prepare his own breakfast burrito based on a toasted flour tortilla filled with white albacore tuna, celery, parsley, tomato, lettuce, sprouts, lemon juice, pepper, mayonnaise and a slathering of hot salsa. My itinerary included Chicago, where *Red Heat* was being filmed, Los Angeles for *Die Hard* with Bruce Willis and *Midnight Run* with Robert De Niro, who ate apart from the crew and favored rice cakes and blackened swordfish, and San Antonio for *Lost Angels* starring among others Cybill Shepard and Donald Sutherland. There the lowest budget for catering resulted in a very unhappy crew, including the director, Hugh Hudson (*Chariots of Fire* and *Greystoke*), who complained loudly about being served chocolate-covered strawberries *on lettuce*.

Hardly in the same category as school, hospital or prison food, location catering, despite the range of choices lavishly laid out on cornucopia buffets, usually for breakfasts and lunches, inspired the same proportion of gripes, whether because there were not enough options for vegans, not enough meat and potatoes for Texans or enough sushi and fruit for Californians. For sheer showmanship the winner was a catering firm partly owned by Francis Ford Coppola, himself a serious gourmand who demanded pizza ovens in vans, china plates, and musical accompaniments matched to menus—accordion players for an Italian *pranzo*, mariachi for a Mexican *comida*. My favorite comment came from James Belushi, who was on a seven-day diet while making *Red Heat*. As I watched him dig into two hamburgers with everything after downing an abstemious turkey sandwich, I asked him how much he had lost, to which he answered, "A whole week."

No story on institutional fare took me on so delightful and exciting an odyssey as my around-the-world survey of airline food for the first issue (September 1987) of *Condé Nast Traveler*. Because of efforts to appeal to an upscale audience, Harry Evans told me to fly business class on as many different airlines as possible and always on flights that would include full meals. It was a strange and costly booking procedure for the travel agent who, because of the requirement of anonymity, could not take advantage of discounts or perks that might be offered to a travel magazine or known food critic.

The itinerary began with a TWA flight from New York to Los Angeles, followed by Continental Airlines to Hawaii, Japan Air Lines to Tokyo, United Airlines to Hong Kong, Qantas Airways to Sydney, Singapore Airlines to Singapore, Air India to Bombay, Lufthansa to Frankfurt, Alitalia to Rome, Swissair to Zurich and Copenhagen and, finally, SAS to New York. Although I could probably have completed the assignment within a week, it seemed prudent to use the money to finance a few other stories, and so it lasted almost three weeks. I stopped for three days each in Singapore (to write about street food) and Sydney and four days in Copenhagen, where Dick joined me and we caught up on local food. But the high-spot was my stop in Tokyo, where I visited the stunning fish market, Tsukiji, at 4:30 in the morning. I watched as a five-hundred-pound bluefin tuna flown in from Montauk was auctioned for $50,000 to a wholesaler who then invited me and my guide and interpreter to watch the cutting. Laid out on a huge dolly, the fish was sliced into vertical quarters with a long, curved saber-like blade and we were invited to try the meat left on the bone frame, a delicacy considered a lagniappe for choice customers. Despite being heavily packed in ice for two days, the rose-red meat was still faintly warm, so large was the fish, and it tasted like the most sublime beef carpaccio imaginable.

My mandate was not only to report on the airline meals but to take record photographs with a Polaroid camera, a task that caused great stir and annoyance to anyone in a neighboring seat, to say nothing of suspicion. I took to mumbling about trying out this new camera for close-range shots so I could learn to focus on folk art specimens that I would be studying. Indeed, that close range proved to be a problem and until I learned to focus, the only subject I recorded was my lap. To complicate things even more, when a choice of two meals was offered—almost standard for business class—I was to try to get both. My tactic was to first request the one I thought would be more popular (beef, for example) and so would run out, then sample it and declare that for one reason or another (too rare, too well-done, too salty,) I couldn't eat it and so would receive the alternate.

Having had so many airline meals and seeing so many of their commissaries, I knew that the main problem in realizing good food was the very limited storage, heating and cooling space aboard planes, and the awkwardness of serving and eating. With an understandably overwhelming concern for food safety, airline caterers keep everything cold, icily so, although heating facilities are less effective. All cold items, including trays, dishes and utensils, are slid into chillers, and food that is heated separately is, unpleasantly enough, added to the ice-cold trays. Budgets for food are so amazingly low that the best ingredients are rarely used to begin with. In no area of institutional food is redesign more essential than in air travel, if, indeed, airlines even continue to serve food, as fewer are doing. The design should begin with the facilities available and work back to the dishes that can be successfully produced under such circumstances, not the other way around. Instead of starting with a complex, traditional dish such as the breaded and fried chicken Kiev and squeezing it through a system that will render it flat, mushy and springing leaks of its butter filling, it would be desirable to consider heating and storing capabilities better suited to some sort of chicken stew or even a credible sandwich. I have always felt that airlines still suffer from having made early comparisons between their food and that of the great ocean liners that had magnificent kitchens and staffs for much longer journeys. Really good sandwiches and salads might seem to be the wisest solution, although surveys have indicated that they would not satisfy relatively unsophisticated passengers who expect hot food for the price of a ticket, especially on flights of more than three hours.

With all of that in mind, I began the first leg of my odyssey aboard TWA on Easter Sunday morning. The flight was three hours late in taking off because of equipment failure, so the food carts holding breakfast were moved from one aircraft to the other, making the meal not only cold and soggy after sitting around for the extra time, but causing the strawberry sauce to spill all over the french toast, rendering it a gooey, syrupy mush. For the most part, I found the business class food on all flights somewhat better than in economy but rarely in proportion to the considerably higher fare. The best meal proved to be aboard a United Airlines flight from Tokyo to Hong Kong. Working my scam on the first choice of filet mignon, I later was given the bento—a pretty lacquer-like plastic box with separate compartments, each holding a different tempting morsel, and all best at room temperature. That sort of small-scale, diverting nibbling proved perfect for a passenger strapped into a seat for many hours and should provide a model for airline meals of any ethnic origin.

I also rated everything else aboard the planes—decor, leg room, seat incline, blankets, personnel uniforms, souvenir giveaways, music programs, movies, washrooms and, of course, staff efficiency and courtesy. Most notably, the least felicitous farewell message came as we were deplaning from Singapore Airlines: "Remember that the penalty for drug traffickers under Singapore law is death." Have a nice day.

"Buy me some peanuts and Crackerjacks" proved to be aesthetically the safest dinner order in baseball parks around the country in the club-restaurants, cafeterias, food courts, and the eats hawked among the seats. Thus did I taste my way through the Baltimore (Orioles), Cincinnati (Reds), Houston (Astros), Arlington (Texas Rangers), Milwaukee (Braves), Los Angeles (Dodgers), Chicago (Cubs and White Sox) and New York (Yankees and Mets). That research left me with the unsurprising knowledge that in general the fare was abysmal and expensive, with poor products poorly mishandled, the most common flaw being the wrapping of hot foods that became steamily washed out. Hot dogs in the food courts tended to be better than those in the stands because the former were grilled and not wrapped. Not wanting to take the time to see so many ball games, I ran all over rounding up the food before and during the first few innings, usually leaving by the third. In Arlington, this proved a great problem, as neither Dick nor I could remember where we had parked our car and we feared that we might have to wait until the game was over and all fans had driven off.

Having no one to keep me company at Dodger Stadium in Los Angeles and fearing that I might not get a taxi back after only three innings, I invited the cab driver who took me there to use my extra ticket and watch the game until I had completed my mission. (My only condition was that he turn off his meter while parked.) A native of Queens and of Italian descent, he was most congenial and gave me his recipe for broccoli di rape with garlic, olive oil and hot peppers ("remember to brown the salt with the garlic") as he complained that it was never done correctly anywhere in the state of California. Imagine my surprise about a year later, when I was again in L.A., and jumped into a cab outside of the Beverly-Wilshire Hotel, and recognized the same driver. He was equally taken aback when I opened with "Feel like going to a ball game this afternoon?"

Saving the best for last, I can report that by far the most delicious institutional spreads I found were on an offshore oil rig in the Gulf of Mexico. Having heard rumors of the superb and copious meals aimed at keeping rig workers placated during their two-week isolation, I managed to get invited to the bright green drilling rig, the Key Manhattan, for a story in *Time*, unaware of the jangling necessity to land in a helicopter on a round platform that from the air looked like a tea tray suspended over an ocean. That, plus the call to the deck a few hours later to see twister-like waterspouts form on the horizon, spiced up the adventure considerably. Not that the perfect food needed added seasoning. Here having homogeneous audience helped a great deal, for the lusty appetites of the male and female rig workers were well satisfied with steaks, roast beef, hamburgers and all sorts of potatoes, macaroni, vegetables and cakes. Since the vast majority of rig workers traditionally come from Louisiana, Texas, Alabama, Tennessee and Mississippi, all have a taste for southern and Creole-Cajun specialties. Aboard the Key Manhattan, the twenty-four-hour meals included delectable versions of red beans and dirty rice, gumbo, crunchy peppered fried chicken, corn bread, biscuits, eggs-any-style with bacon and hot smoky sausage and, on the day I was there, a luscious black-eyed pea jambalaya, for which the cook generously gave me the recipe.

That I continue my research on institutional food still hopeful that I will find places where it is being well done may just represent a triumph of optimism over experience.

Matters of Taste

I Eat Hot!

"YOU WILL NOT LIKE THE PEOPLE IN SICHUAN," warned Guoping Fei, my invaluable interpreter and guide throughout a month-long gastronomic tour of China in 1986, on assignment from *Time* magazine.

"Why not?" I asked.

"Because they eat hot. People who eat hot shout and have bad tempers. Deng Xiaoping was born in Sichuan and Mao Zedong was from Hunan—both provinces where food is full of peppercorns and hot chilies. You eat pretty hot, too, so you will have big arguments." Had I known it then, I could have told him that those who eat hot are also considered thrill seekers who deliberately

take limited risks, something I learned from Dr. Paul Rozin and
Deborah Schiller, experts in taste perceptions at the University of
Pennsylvania. Among the limited risks they incur are riding roller
coasters, taking hot baths and gambling, the last being the one that
has never appealed to me.

By the time we approached the Sichuan city of Chengdu, Fei
and I had traveled through Shanghai, Suzhou, Hangzhou, Nanjing,
Beijing and Xi'an. He had had time to realize not only that I liked
hotly seasoned food but that I was pretty determined, insisting on
seeing only what I wanted to see and skipping the rest, which might
include climbing soaring staircases to rooftops and monuments
only to look down, or visiting yet another museum dedicated to the
socialist realist glories of the Maoist regime. The local guides who
met us in each city were reluctant to deviate from their authorita-
tively typed itineraries ("It cannot be changed. It is typed . . ."),
and so Fei diplomatically cajoled and explained why I preferred to
spend time at museums devoted to fine arts and provincial crafts, to
street food vendors, restaurants and markets and institutional food
in hospitals, schools and workers' cafeterias. For all the Chinese I
knew, he might have been telling them that I was a crazy but
important journalist who was to be humored, but as long as it
worked, who cared? In fact, it was indeed a rare stroke of luck that
made Fei my guide.

That I was in China at all was due to Henry Grunwald, then the
editor in chief of *Time-Life* magazines and who with managing
editor Ray Cave had invited me to join *Time* when I left the *New
York Times*. I am often asked if I have ever regretted leaving the
Times. Not only is the answer never, not even once, but also that
this trip to China was enough to have made my leaving worthwhile.

Travel had always been the lure for me. Whether I proposed
stories about home furnishings or food, my aim was to think up
ideas that would take me to some far-off place. I had been quite

successful in that before going to the *Times* but once there was confined to reviewing restaurants in New York. In my eight years on staff there were only a few assignments abroad, including two to France and one to Italy, and occasional short swings to cities such as Chicago, New Orleans, Washington, D.C., Austin and Los Angeles.

For years I had drawn upon my travels in evaluating foreign food products and cuisines as they emerged here, but I began to feel that my experiences had been exhausted and that my references were no longer valid. I was therefore pleased to travel again and refresh my thoughts and ideas about food and the life and customs surrounding it. There are many handles by which one can pick up a foreign culture, and food is surely one of the most engaging and rewarding, partly because of exchanges with locals in restaurants, but also when visiting markets, farms or processors of one sort or another. I have found the subject of food to be special, as local people generally relax and trust strangers when they speak of their native food, feeling more open when they meet on this common and benign ground.

There was no country that I wanted to roam around in more than China, a destination that had so far eluded me. I had long considered the Chinese cuisine to be the world's most intricate, ingenious, varied and dramatic—even though we cannot sample the full depth and breadth of it here. That view is shared by many chefs I have met, as well as by Craig Claiborne in the days when we were speaking. Henry Grunwald asked me to go to China after a visit there during which, he said, he never had a good meal. He wanted to know why the meals were so badly prepared, what had happened to the old culinary traditions and if there was any really good food to be found. A devout European in all of his preferences, the Vienna-born Grunwald may have been skeptical about Chinese food anyway, and I heard he had blanched when he received my postcard reading, "Who says there's no good food in China? Only today I had camel's lips, snake soup and sea slugs. Wish you were here." The northern Chinese say that their countrymen to the south eat everything that flies except airplanes and everything with legs except tables. To outsiders, that description holds for all of China, and I firmly believe that a good Chinese chef can make even an airplane or a table taste wonderful.

Travel to China was not easy in those days, and as the quota for visiting journalists had already been filled for that year, I had to find an accredited Chinese organization to host and arrange my trip. Through a series of contacts, my host became the Shanghai International Culture Association and so I began in Shanghai, where I was met by Fei. Having been warned about often sleazy accommodations, I brought the suggested pillowcase, sheet and bath towel, all of which I soon found unnecessary and left with the *Time* staff in Beijing. Much more useful were the many pairs of disposable chopsticks I had from my local sushi restaurant, and the miniature airline bottles of vodka gathered during my business-class flights that I used to rinse out questionable cups and bowls. Fei and I happily shared them as we sampled the endlessly tempting street foods by night and day, whether the spicy Sichuan noodles that were twisted and stretched in skeins and splayed out into strands before our eyes in Chengdu's night food market, or the half-steamed, half-fried potstickers explosively steaming as they were uncovered in woks at an open-air stall in Suzhou. On trains, most Chinese passengers carried their own metal teacups, and in an employee cafeteria I saw workers using bowls brought from home, all attempts to avoid hepatitis and other gastrointestinal demons, none of which attacked me. The only ingredient that irritated my digestion was the cheap, stale cooking oil commonly used in many tourist hotel restaurants, and the air filled with fumes from the soft coal fuel so irritated my throat that by the time I left, I could hardly speak. I was offended aesthetically by many foods, such as the Spam-like meat used to replicate delicate rose petals in cold appetizers, or canned meats and vegetables swimming in grease, especially if served at a banquet that cost $375 for eight, the minimum number one could book even if only four appeared. Booking, by the way, was an all-day affair, as Fei assured me we had to keep checking back to be sure our reservations were noted through shift changes.

Although I like all of China's regional cuisines, my favorites are those of Guangzhou (Canton), Sichuan and Hunan. Among the Sichuanese dishes, my benchmark is mapo dofu (pock-marked old woman's bean curd, honoring the pock-marked woman who created the dish). It is an incendiary stir-fry of creamy soft white bean curd (dofu), ground pork, silken tree ear mushrooms, crisp water chestnuts, peanuts, scallions, ginger, garlic and enough of Sichuan's *huajiao* peppercorns and chilies (whole and in paste) to flambé even an asbestos-lined palate. Despite the heat, it is to me the sort of sustaining comfort food I crave in times of stress, as I do linguine with white clam sauce, fried eggs with almost-burned rye toast, homemade chicken noodle soup or warm, buttery Rome Beauty apples baked with cinnamon sugar. I vowed to order mapo dofu wherever I found it in China to try different versions and decide which was best.

Coincidentally, our first lunch was in the Sichuan restaurant of the handsome old Jinjiang Hotel in Shanghai. Because I wanted to find out as much as possible about the state of Chinese cookery, I was not anonymous but rather shared the table with members of tourist and cultural organizations and the venerable master chef Hu Yulu, who had come out of retirement to run this kitchen, where he trained young cooks. He invited me to order from a Chinese-English menu and politely complimented my choices before adding a few of his own. To my selections of pungent cold cabbage, hot

and sour soup, cold sesame-flavored eggplant, chicken with chilies
and peanuts, a whole fried carp glossed with chili oil and the mapo
dofu, he added kidneys in cold sesame sauce, long-life noodles,
dry-sautéed string beans and double-cooked pork. The meal was
spectacularly good and resonated during the rest of my trip. For
one thing, I was to be frustrated in my search because the Jinjiang
Hotel's mapo dofu proved to be the ultimate, making for many disappointments in other versions. That lunch also proved a landmark
experience for Fei and provided a leitmotif for our journey. A
native of Shanghai, where gently sweet and flowery flavors prevail
in dishes such as white-cooked shrimp, eel with slivered leeks and
rice-studded lion's head meatballs, he was gasping and blotting up
the chili oil on his palate with rice throughout our meal. Never had
he eaten such hotly seasoned food. Gradually, however, as we visited other Sichuan restaurants, he began to get used to it and by the
time we reached Chengdu, he complained if a dish was not hot
enough. Although he had traveled around the country with many
visitors, none had eating as the prime agenda, and he gained about
ten pounds as we progressed. (Now living in Albany, New York,
with his wife and daughter, he reports that he has mastered the art
of cooking mapo dofu.)

The most insightful thing I learned from Hu Yulu was that the
main reason for the decline in the Chinese cuisine was the Cultural
Revolution, during which any efforts at embellishment were regarded as signs of bourgeois decadence, a convenient philosophy
when food was disastrously scarce. The best chefs fled to Hong
Kong, Bangkok, Singapore, Australia, Canada and the United
States, creating not only a shortage of talent but leaving an entire
generation with no taste memory of the country's much revered
culinary traditions. A year or two before my visit, however, the
government had awakened to the blessings of capitalism (encoded
in the Chinese DNA, I suspect) and realized the need to restore the

country's cuisine, and so it entered into joint ventures with hotels and restaurateurs abroad and were welcoming back old master chefs to do stints as teachers. This, despite still existing food shortages so severe that most working people, including Fei, subsisted solely on street food by day, and those wanting to provide their families with fresh fish, chicken and vegetables other than cabbages and onions went to the markets between four and five A.M., lest the best ingredients be gone. One morning I slipped out of my Shanghai hotel at 4:30, before Fei arrived, and followed in reverse the trail of men and women carrying vegetables, live chickens or ducks with their feet tied, and living carp in plastic bags of water until I reached the typically teeming, stiflingly odoriferous market that was a wonderland of exotica, as all Chinese food markets turned out to be. Among them, my favorites were those in Chengdu (because of medicinal ingredients like dried snakes and turtle shells and mounds of mysteriously scented spices), and the Qingping market in Guangzhou, mostly for the aquarium aspects of the live fish section and the endless lanes of stalls displaying gnarled brown roots of fresh ginger, enough, one would think, to keep the whole world in ginger for a year, but not so where that spice replaces our lemon to lend a modifying astringency to fish.

The subtle, gentle cuisine of South China's Canton region with its well-balanced flavors was until about twenty-five years ago the only regional Chinese food generally available in the United States. Like the southern cooking of India and Italy, it was considered inexpensive and as such was often carelessly prepared. To erase that image and make it possible to charge higher prices in more elaborate settings, the northern cuisines of China, such as Beijing with its Mandarin cooking, and the spicier foods of Hunan and Sichuan were introduced, just as the specialties of northern India and Italy were for the same reasons. Recently, however, the food of Canton is returning to favor with its subtly soothing yet flavorful dishes such as lobster, shrimp or crabs in black bean sauce, its ginger and scallion steamed fish (often caught live from window tanks when ordered), the wonton dumplings and, one of my favorites, steamed ground pork and water chestnuts crowned with a salted duck egg.

As usual, it was the human contacts that remain the most memorable, especially in Shanghai at the Speakers' Corner in a large park. Chinese students learning English gathered there to engage English-speaking tourists in conversations on all sorts of subjects. Fei kept me moving in proper time from one group to another, partly to field questions about workers' conditions in the United States (generally far better than those in China, I explained, couching my remarks carefully), but even more about the education and opportunities for young people and American music. In those days, our folk singers were the favorites and many were Stephen Foster fans. That fit the times in every way, for the Mao era of plainness still prevailed, with girls and women wearing no makeup and dressing drably and austerely. I never once saw a young couple holding hands or otherwise showing affection in public.

Most of my personal contacts naturally were in the food world. One day in Shanghai we decided not to use our car and driver and midday were overtaken by a torrential rain that showed no signs of abating. Taxis were impossible to find and so Fei stashed me inside a food shop until he could reach a telephone (scarce in those days) and call our driver. It was a general food store that included a bakery where moon cakes were being prepared for the autumn Moon Festival. I watched six women shape the high, round pastry buns, fill them with a sort of mincemeat, fold them closed and then stamp the tops in a red dye with calligraphy and good luck symbols. After about five minutes, one worker handed me the wooden stamp and indicated that I should make myself useful by marking buns. Of course, I did, and we all worked in unison without speaking for about half an hour, but with a sense of fun and friendship.

Many chefs befriended me and invited me to observe classes in dicing and slicing the Chinese way, and I had a lesson in making soup dumplings in the Jinfeng Baozi café in Beijing. The chef guided me in stretching the soft dough, cupping it and filling it with seasoned ground pork sometimes mixed with crabmeat, then pinching the top closed halfway to form a pouch before trickling in hot broth from a teapot. Finally the top was twisted closed and the dumplings were steamed. The next part of the lesson was even more difficult—eating each hot, juicy bun all at once, picking it up with a china spoon and chopsticks and not letting it break open so soup could leak out before the dumpling was in my mouth. With enough luck and skill, I did not scald my tongue.

Another cherished encounter was with Chef Zhan Qinbiao at the Songhelou restaurant in Suzhou. We had had a memorable time together a few years before in New York while I was still at the *Times*. He was sent by the Chinese government to cook for twenty-six Chinese craftsmen and honchos who were installing a Ming garden in the Metropolitan Museum of Art, the gift of Brooke Astor. An old friend, Bunny Heller, then in the museum's press office, suggested that I do a story about the chef and sample his food at a banquet he would prepare for eight of us. Accepting immediately, I went shopping with him, then spent the day watching and noting as he cooked our dinner, which turned out to be as delectable as we had expected.

To show appreciation (and to have fun), I invited Zhan Qinbiao, his overseers and some museum staff to two dinners—one at the Palm and the other at the Coach House. While they were fascinated by both, it was the Palm that won the chef, because the basically short-order kitchen, where steaks, chops and lobsters are grilled, and side dishes are cooked in thin metal skillets over flaming heat, appealed instantly, being very similar to his own cooking methods. In a few minutes, he began frying and flipping hash brown potatoes and tossing spinach with garlic and olive oil, and though all understood the importance of beef here, they were unused to large chunks of it and ate dutifully if not completely. Their preferences were for those potatoes and the linguine in a mild tomato and clam sauce. At the Coach House, they were won over by crab cakes, fried chicken and cornsticks and took some American cornmeal to experiment with when back in China.

I therefore contacted Zhan Qinbiao, telling him when I would be in Suzhou, and he met us at the train, showed us through food markets and gardens and along the all-too-fragrant canals of his city, and then dished up an exquisite Suzhou meal at his restaurant. The food of that region is even more softly sweet and aromatic than Shanghai's. We had winter melon soup steamed and served in a carved melon, baby bok choy looking like pale jade polliwogs as they nestled under earthy black mushrooms, sesame- and garlic-scented fried slivers of eel, and Suzhou's famous squirrel fish—a whole fish scored in a diamond pattern before being fried, causing the skin to stand in furry points and accompanied by a sweet-sour sauce that softens flavor and texture.

Guangzhou, then the most capitalistic city in China, also had the best hotels and food that included a rich congee—the breakfast rice porridge that is most elegant when made with crabmeat, flecks of pickled garlic and ginger. Continuing to Taiwan, where I had never been, I was struck by the sharp contrast in professional service in restaurants as well as by the finesse in preparation and the abundance of high-quality foods. It was an indication to me that personal financial incentive seems to inspire the best efforts.

Modernized Beijing and Xi'an were almost unrecognizable when I returned in 2001, except at their most traditional sights (the terracotta soldiers in Xi'an and the palaces, monuments and museums of

Beijing). That is definitely good news for many Chinese, who understandably would trade antique charm for indoor plumbing, but the unavoidable homogenization does make travel a little less interesting. It is still possible to turn a corner here or there and glimpse the graceful old low houses with gray tile roofs set around inner courtyard gardens, and to see the morning activity of occupants brushing teeth, shaving, scaling fish and trimming vegetables on the street, but anyone who wants to see that had better get to China in a hurry. Such relics are being cleared for modern apartments throughout the country, a project much hastened for the 2012 Olympics. And in Shanghai, as I write, a clever and charming Chinese-American lawyer, Handel C. H. Lee, who already owns the excellent Courtyard Gallery Restaurant in Beijing, is readying a remodeled landmark building on the old Shanghai Bund to house four restaurants led by several superstar chefs, foremost among them Jean-Georges Vongerichten, expected to open in the spring of 2004.

Fortunately, food and service in 2001 had improved tremendously, the high spots being Mongolian lamb and noodle specialties in the Muslim night market of Xi'an, and the array of just about every food on skewers in the street stalls of Beijing, where I also had a benchmark Beijing (a.k.a. Peking) duck, its crisp skin sprinkled with crystals of coarse sugar, a style served to women, whose palates long ago were decreed too delicate to withstand the usual five-spice salt that includes star anise and pepper.

Perhaps the biggest surprise on my return to Beijing was that the dreary dishes and drab decors of the Mao era had become a stylish retro trend, just as we make periodic retreats to the foods and artifacts of the Great Depression or the fifties.

Back home at *Vanity Fair*, the challenge was to come up with story ideas that would appeal to Tina Brown, who graciously and however painfully lived out the contract I had signed with her predecessor Leo Lerman. "Painfully," because her interest in food apparently began and ended with Diet Pepsi. Still I think she enjoyed my report "The Ten Most Overrated Restaurants in America" almost as much as I enjoyed doing it, primarily because it predictably made the sort of waves we both delighted in. And though my attempt to take Orson Welles to Paris for lunch fell through because, the great impresario told me, he had a better offer to travel there to make a film, I did get an exciting interview with Federico Fellini over lunch in Rome, which I reported on.

About a year later, Tina's husband, Harry Evans, started *Condé Nast Traveler,* for which I began to write and select each year the fifty U.S. restaurants I considered to be "worth a special journey." I was reluctant to dub them the "best," as that implied that I had gone to every restaurant in the country, but that is the way the public always read it.

Writing for the *Traveler* was pure joy, at least as long as Harry Evans was in charge. It is always difficult to work for someone who is insecure, waffling and susceptible to every passing influence, but for a freelancer it is sheer hell because decisions are made when you are not around and are presented fait accompli. Evans was anything but that, being bold enough to take expensive chances and a superstar editor much in charge. In addition, he was generous with praise, something no writer (or anyone else) fails to appreciate.

Among the many surprises that I noted while covering Europe and the United States was the gradual disappearance of local cuisines, or if not disappearance then a kind of fashionable updating that generally rendered them innocuous. This was as sadly true in Copenhagen in 1986 as it continues to be in Chicago today. It was becoming difficult to find the wonderful Danish dishes I had loved in 1960. Although excellent open-face sandwiches—smørrebrød— were still to be had, as were the arrays of enticing herrings, main dishes such as bacon and egg pancakes, beefsteak topped with parsley butter and poached corned duckling with frozen cream horseradish were served in only a few obscure spots.

Similarly, although Chicago still has some good rib joints, I have found none that compares to the raffish outposts that lined Rush Street nor a steak house to match the bygone Stockyards Inn, where one branded a steak of choice—now, perhaps, not quite PC among the squeamish set. New Orleans held out longer than any other major city, making it dearer to my heart than it was for so many other reasons that include the deliciously seedy *déshabillé* of the French Quarter and the laissez-faire life-style, more reminiscent of a Spanish colonial outpost than of Paris. For a long time, locals were too satisfied with and proud of their own specialties to try many others.

What I began to realize as I traveled is that there are two different points of view in evaluating a city's restaurants. One is that of the locals, who understandably want to try food of other places that they have read about or discovered when traveling. The visitor, on the other hand, wants (or should want) to try the food that can only be had in a particular place—native fare on home ground that helps define the true travel experience, which is getting harder to find every day. A New Orleanian may well want to have some Chinese, real Italian (as compared to New Orleans–Italian, best realized at Mosca's) or Middle Eastern cooking, but I would no more waste time on those places than I would by ordering gumbo in Shanghai. Only occasionally have I found restaurants serving extraordinary examples of cuisines foreign to their areas and so well worth visiting. Among such were the bygone, much lamented Le Français when it was run by its gifted French chef Jean Banchet in Wheeling, Illinois, the fine Indian-French fusion Restaurant Raji, created by the late Raji Jallepalli in Memphis, Tennessee, many sushi bars in Los Angeles, some Vietnamese and Moroccan restaurants in Paris, and three Italian trattorias in Beirut, Lebanon, when I visited in 1960. For the rest, I say, when in Paris, Munich or Austin do not eat as the Romans do.

That food provides clues to the history and lore of an area is nowhere more obvious than in Alto-Adige, the part of northern Italy that was known as the South Tyrol and belonged to Austria before World War I, and which Dick and I visited in 1992. Dishes such as ravioli filled with bloodwurst or cotechino sausage served on sauerkraut and veal cutlet Milanese double-billed as wiener schnitzel announce this is indeed an Italo-Austrian area, as did pizzerias known as pizzastuben. All signs and written material appeared in two languages and each city, such as the enchanting Merano, had two mayors, one who campaigned in Italian, the other in German. Leaving the stunning Hotel Mozart, the black-and-white Secessionist masterpiece inspired by the designs of Josef Hoffmann and sadly no longer in existence, we drove through mountain passes and towns, meeting with restaurateurs and producers of incomparable hams and bacons to find that those over fifty or sixty preferred to speak German, chiding their twenty-something offspring who opted for Italian, their parents longing, no doubt, for the good old days.

No trip in search of good food was more enlightening than the one we took to Israel in 1994. Advance reports were of dreadful food ineptly served, with breakfast being the only over-the-top buffet meal that visitors stoked up on to see them through the day. The reason for such reports, as I discovered, was that they were mainly based on visits to French, Italian and Chinese eating places that were indeed dreadful. That left a whole exotic choice of cuisines including the subtly spiced dishes of Yemen, Morocco, Tunisia, Bukhara, Iraq, Iran and Egypt, to say nothing of the diverse and supple breads and the Arab-Israeli menu of burnished kebobs holding bits of meat, sweetbreads or foie gras, the soothing sesame-accented chickpea dip, hummus, the garlic-etched baba

gannoujh based on smoky eggplant or the crisp falafel bean croquettes so satisfying with yogurt and chopped scallions puffing out
grainy pita. All were delectably well represented in many places,
albeit with service most kindly described as naïve. All also celebrated the diverse ethnicity of the country, matching our own.

Similarly in Hungary, Czechoslovakia and Poland in 1992, I
found so-called Continental food a complete waste of time, money
and calories, but found more than enough solace in their hefty,
truly hot soups and juicy, crisp-skinned duck and goose triumphs,
and although I am not generally a devotee of sweets, I couldn't
resist the fragrant fried yeast crullers the Poles call *panczki,* most
famously made at the Warsaw bakery of A. Blikle, or Budapest's
strudels and coffee cakes and especially *pogásca,* salt-flavored biscuits that are teasingly dry, something my grandmother used to
make. My grandmother also came back in full force in Cracow,
where I ordered hot beet borscht that turned out to be as clear as
liquid rubies and scented with crushed black peppercorns and garlic, a soup I had not tasted since I had it at my grandmother's and
one I worked hard to duplicate when I wrote *From My Mother's
Kitchen.* That trip to Eastern Europe provided a bonus in taking
me to Bialystok, Poland, where I began my research on the history
of that city's famed bialy onion roll and of the Jews who used to
live there, resulting in *The Bialy Eaters.*

For the most part, however, I was pleased to tour the United
States, gathering material for *Condé Nast Traveler* to write monthly
columns and to choose the year's fifty most interesting restaurants.
As a lover of cities, preferring them to natural landscapes, I would
rather take a vacation in any great city than on any cruise or in any
resort, no matter how glamorous or posh—and boring. Therefore,
I welcomed the six years during which I could revisit favorite cities
and see many I had missed. Those travels were also useful because
I had started a newsletter, *Mimi Sheraton's Taste,* a monthly

devoted to restaurants in New York but with recommendations for other cities as well. Dick and I worked on it for three successful years, but as the 1987 recession took hold, we saw that renewals would be costly to come by and so we ended it while we were ahead.

During those six years, it was exciting to sense again the fresh and open brashness of Chicago, which I consider the first truly American metropolis, New York being a European extension. With its ocean-like Lake Michigan, stunning modern architecture and Art Institute, it had beguiled me since I began going there in 1950 to cover furniture markets twice a year while at *Seventeen*. Good things have always happened to me in the city with the big shoulders, mostly because family connections developed, as my brother, Arthur Solomon, went to the University of Chicago and stayed for the rest of his life to form a law firm with his wife, Lois, and partner, Ray Behrendt. Years later, my son, Marc, attended law school at the same university, so it seemed that there always was someone dear to me in that city.

Dear, too, were newer restaurants such as the New York transplant Coco Pazzo, Kiki's Bistro with its Provençale menu, and Topolobampo and Frontera Grill run by the inventive chef Rick Bayless, and Jacky Pluton's very authentic Jacky's Bistro in Evanston almost can make me forget other old-time favorites. Almost, because it would take a lot to replace the stylish Imperial House, known for black mushroom consommé and french fried strawberries with zabayon sauce, or the Pump Room of the Ambassador Hotel, where flaming shashlik brandished by turbaned waiters lit up the glamorous room, or Don-the-Beachcomber, one of the earliest outposts of a pseudo-Polynesian cuisine based on Chinese food with pineapple and coconut, and succulent pupu appetizers washed down with opulently intoxicating drinks shaded by little paper parasols.

In New Orleans, Galatoire's remains a must stop at least once during each trip so that I can indulge in fried eggplant, shrimp remoulade, oysters and bacon en brochette and pompano mcunière almondine. I am never there without recalling the late Alan Jaffe, friend and founder of the French Quarter jazz mecca Preservation Hall, who tried to convince me that there was a place for canned peas and that they were the "right" ingredient in that restaurant's chicken Clemenceau. All I kept thinking was, "This would be better with fresh peas." I never could fault Alan, however, for the five-hour lunch he arranged at Buster Holmes, a down-at-the-heels bar on the corner of Orleans and Burgundy, where we began lunch at 11:30 in the morning with about ten people, eating our way slowly through earthy red beans and rice, fried chicken showered with garlic, crunchy fried shrimp and peppery oysters, Buster's incomparable soft and tender meatballs, boiled and fried crawfish, stuffed eggplant and perhaps more. Commander's Palace is a place I liked best when Emeril Lagasse was the chef, but I still get delicious food there when I am recognized. If I have found new favorites such as Emeril's, Nola's and Susan Spicer's Bayona, it is because their cooking, however inventive, reflects the Louisiana spirit and tastes "right" in that milieu.

The part of the country I knew least about was the Southwest. I was captivated by New Mexico and Arizona, both of which bowled me over with their desert landscapes, the unbelievable eerie beauty of cactus and, in Sedona, with monumental red mountains so subtly sculptured and theatrical that I could not believe they were not man-made. Also man-made in Santa Fe were the comforting dishes incorporating many ingredients of the local native Americans, such as the soup-stew of the dried white corn, posole, as served at the Shed, and the Mexican-informed breakfast burritos that I could have eaten all day long at Café Pasqual. In Tucson, I favored the authentic, spare Mexican fare at the little Mi Nidito rather than fashionable food at more stylish places, and also in Tucson, I loved the smoky Indian fry bread sold on Sunday outside the old San Xavier del Bac Mission. Phoenix with its lavish gardens and elaborate homes in guarded compounds looked more like Beverly Hills than Arizona so I was not surprised by the sophistication of the dishes at Christopher's and at Vincent's on Camelback. Given my taste for hotly seasoned food, however, the spot that really spoke to me was Los Dos Molinos, where a fusion of Southwestern flavors included enough hot chilies to make me almost as intransigent as Deng Xiaoping or Mao.

We Eat What We Are

"BY THEIR EATING HABITS, ye shall know them" may not be a biblical admonition, but it has become part of my own religious canon. Observing fellow diners throughout the years when we were almost always four at table (unless we were six or eight for a Chinese or Indian meal), I noted their telltale idiosyncracies of likes and dislikes and prejudices.

That is a phenomenon well understood by perceptive filmmakers who use food as props to delineate character. The most outstanding example in my recollection appears in Martin Scorsese's film *Taxi Driver*, when the self-hating hack, Travis Bickle as played by Robert De Niro, eats only junk food such as fast-food burgers, candy and white bread soaked in milk and peach brandy. When he finally manages a lunch date in a restaurant with his much-admired golden girl (Cybill Shepherd), he looks perplexed as she orders a salad. Hesitating in embarrassed desperation over what dish would seem suitably classy, he chooses apple pie. In another scene, he takes a young prostitute (Jodie Foster) to breakfast, and we watch her spread a thick layer of grape jelly on to white bread and then shower it with sugar before folding it over. Wondering how anyone could have invented such bizarre and degrading food, I asked the film's writer, Paul Schrader. He said that he had actually known drug addicts who ate the bread-milk-peach brandy concoction and that he and Scorsese once took a young whore to breakfast and she prepared that exact bread-jelly-sugar sandwich. The message, clearly, was "junk food, junk people."

Less menacing, the types I came to recognize at my table were the Reluctants, usually health- or diet-conscious women who came along for the glamour of being part of a review, or because their husbands really wanted to, or just because we were friends and I needed bodies to try enough dishes. As I indicated their options for ordering, explaining that they had to have the dish the chef's way and could not request their swordfish without butter or oil or other similar culinary obscenities, invariably they expressed displeasure either with an outright form of "yech" or with what they assumed was an inaudible sucking in of breath and tightening of lips. After distributing overly generous samples of their portions to me and anyone else who was interested, the eternal dieters would push the food around on the plate, scattering it to seemingly reduce its mass. It is a trick I recognized from childhood, when I did the same with much hated peas and lima beans, only to watch my mother regroup them and point out how little I had eaten. When pasta was ubiqui-tous and had to be sampled for reviews, the calorie-watchers would have a taste or two, and then carefully pick off and eat only the sauce. In a most unforgettable incident one such woman, who was a health-oriented food writer and sometime restaurant critic, grimaced openly when presented with an exquisite cold half lobster I had asked her to order.

Many Reluctants began every meal by reciting what I have come to call "the Most Amazing Grace," in which they apologized for what they were about to order. "I didn't have a big dinner last night and ate no breakfast today, so I can have the pasta and cheesecake for lunch." Or "I had the swordfish, so I can have the chocolate cake for dessert and I won't eat tomorrow." It is an American litany, still mumbled at almost any meal when I am with anyone other than Dick, a sort of advance confession of gustatory sin to absolve their bodies of calories. It is also phenomenally boring.

Similarly, I knew three cooking school teachers and three practicing food writers who if not anorexic, surely were bulimic. Never did I or others I have asked see one of these scraggly, bone-thin creatures swallow a mouthful of food, not even the cooking teachers during classes that I observed. In addition, most were workout fanatics: joggers, weight lifters, crunchers and treadmill addicts. As I understand anorexia, it is not unusual for sufferers to obsessively prepare food for others, and teaching or writing on the subject could be another form of feeding. All of this is not to say that only the overweight make convincing food critics, tasting and leaving being not only acceptable but wise, even if I never could quite manage that myself. As for exercise, acceptable forms to me include turning the pages of a book, beating egg whites with a wire whisk, spinning a salad dryer, walking and window shopping in New York and climbing the three flights of stairs in my house as necessary.

Returning to the reviewing table, there were the Grabbers, who always ordered the most expensive items of those I indicated, and their choices narrowed as the visits to a particular restaurant progressed. Only caviar was out of bounds unless it was a specialty of the house as at Petrossian, in which case Dick and I went alone, as expensive duplication was unnecessary, or if caviar was part of a preparation, such as blinis. The most egregious Grabber was the husband of a colleague at the *Times,* who finished one main course of roasted chicken with mashed potatoes and some vegetables, and then asked if he could order a steak. Always happy to see an extra dish, I said yes, although I was relieved that no one else at the table followed suit. Grabbers also were usually Guzzlers, quaffing Dick's generally terrific wine choices as though they were water, thereby making a second bottle an unnecessary expense.

Then there were the Indecisives, those who took forever to order, and occasionally, the Joker—invariably male—who asked what would happen if he did not order what I wanted to see, or wouldn't share for a tasting. My answer was that he would pay for his own meal, a threat that always brought the most recalcitrant around. Sometimes the Joker was a helpful soul who tried to bait waiters on my behalf to provoke an incident that I could recount in salty prose, thereby "showing them." Other so-called friends turned out to be Inside Dopes who dined out on their experiences with me, gossiping widely long before my review was published, and who were nevermore invited, if indeed I ever spoke to them again.

There also was the group Dick and I referred to as the Alright-niks. If I did not want to be recognized, neither did I want to invite guests who were in any way intimidating or prepossessing because of face, dress or personal style that might prompt special attention. The Alrightniks, however superb as friends, dressed decently but most unstylishly, suggesting perhaps that they belonged to the bridge-and-tunnel crowd. Unbeknownst to them, I invited or, more candidly, used them at restaurants I suspected of being snooty, to ascertain how they were treated and seated. These unwitting shills were compensated with dinners at some of our very best French, Italian and cutting-edge fusion restaurants.

Being human, I have my own personal peeves, now as then, and much magnified when I spent so much time watching others eat. I mark as unknowing those who order big, ice-cold drinks like Bloody Marys before a dinner that will include wine, and, along the same lines, those who end a meal with cappuccino, basically coffee-flavored hot milk best drunk at breakfast or as a mid-afternoon restorative. I try to turn my eyes away from table companions who chew with their mouths open or who cut long pasta strands with a knife to make them manageable, or who butter an entire slice of bread, then fold and eat it all at once. Then there may be the uncouth eater who, when facing fried eggs at breakfast or brunches, first consumes the white, then puts the entire yolk in his or her mouth and pops it inside, a thought that sends a shudder through me even as I write. Because I like hot foods and beverages to be very, very hot, I get nervous watching slow eaters whose soup or coffee grows cold before my eyes. "Eat quickly," I refrain from saying. "It's getting cold!"

That is, in fact, one of the only gustatory points of contention between Dick and me. "Your mouth must be asbestos lined," he admonishes, as I invariably finish my coffee long before he starts his.

"If you wanted iced coffee, why didn't you ask for it?" I counter. "Don't you know that your coffee just died? It stopped breathing . . ."

As with coffee, so with soup, and Dick would have had sweet revenge had he been with me one winter's day in Helsinki, when the Finnish capital was frosted white and frozen solid. Having spent the morning struggling with a frozen ballpoint pen and camera shutter as I tried to report on the open-air harbor food market, I escaped for lunch into a Russian restaurant, Troika. Desperate to thaw out, I ordered Soldier's Shchi, a soup that contained pungent

sauerkraut, fatty cuts of beef, marrow bones, plump kielbasa
sausage, bacon drippings and root vegetables. It arrived in a covered earthenware casserole and when I raised the lid, a mushroom
cloud of steam wafted upward. Not hesitating, I took a spoonful
and almost cried out. It was the hottest soup I ever have had in my
life, the grease from the meats having formed a scalding top layer.
(Some might say it was too hot, but not me. Still, there definitely
was that small blister on my upper lip.) Being alone, I was embarrassed to show discomfort and so quickly sipped some icy vodka
before continuing to eat more judiciously.

This episode brought back memories of a similar predicament
when I was alone in Bangkok and went to a very authentic Thai
restaurant where I ordered the hottest green curry, assuring the
waiter I did not want it tempered to the tourist palate. That time, I
think I almost died, not being able to catch my breath for what
seemed like an hour. An onlooking guest noticed my crimson face
and tearing eyes, and he rescued me by advising that I not drink
water or beer, which would spread the fiery oils around my mouth,
but rather sop them up with plain rice.

While traveling alone and speaking to strangers, I became
aware that conversations about food inspired confidence and
friendliness. I thought talking about food might be a technique for
interviewing celebrities in fields other than food who shared strong
opinions about cooking and eating, and so might inadvertently
reveal some interesting character traits. Through the years, this
proved to be true for interviews that appeared primarily in the *New
York Times* and *Vanity Fair*.

Revealing his penchant for French food when eating out for special occasions, John Updike admitted to being most at home with
the plain food of New England and the various types of sausages he
grew up with in Pennsylvania Dutch country. "Lebanon bologna is
the most famous, but I prefer the Lehigh type that has more pepper.

The last thing I always have before leaving home is peanut butter spread on a cracker, and even though it's not very good, I eat all the food at literary lunches when I speak because I was raised poor and can't resist free food."

Marveling at the aplomb of a well-dressed woman who twirled green fettuccine onto her fork as we had lunch at Lutèce, he said she looked like "a praying mantis roving the twigs of a creosote bush." Claiming to feel more at home with the food he created for his fictional Harry "Rabbit" Angstrom than for his New York Jewish writer Henry Bech, Updike said that he rarely cooked. "I don't like meat to look like animals. I like it ground up and formed. I used to make meatloaf. You can leave something in, take something out and trim it to a precise shape. You can have ideas about meatloaf." Somehow it all sounded a lot like the way he might plan a novel.

After endless pleas to press agents, and with the help of Leo Lerman, formerly the editor of *Vanity Fair*, I finally had lunch with Federico Fellini in the penthouse restaurant of the Hassler Hotel in Rome. Speaking to one of his handlers in Italian, thinking I would not understand, he said he did not want to sit with the light behind him because it would accent his thinning hair. Once settled, he described in almost touching detail the "sweet and gentle flavors of the past" that he remembered from the small pastel confections made by convent nuns. With a pixieish glint in his eye, he said the dish he missed most from childhood was the dessert trifle the Italians call *zuppa inglese* as his grandmother prepared it. It was a lost flavor, he said, because to pipe on the whipped cream topping, she folded a cone out of a newspaper long out of business. Fellini felt that the ink from that paper lent a special accent, never to be recaptured by the *Corriere della Sera*. He also admitted to hating pasta but loving rice, and when he was told that the kitchen did not have rice with which to make risotto, he pronounced the place "Stupida!" After the story appeared,

I was told that he was embarrassed because I had repeated his remark about the Hassler kitchen.

Various fashion designers talking about food expressed views, not too surprisingly, that related closely to their taste in the clothes they designed. Geoffrey Beene, justly celebrated for his elegant fabrics and the respect he shows them in the simplest handling, emphasized the beauty of ingredients as the starting point for dishes that he loved. When I lunched with Issey Miyake in the SoHo restaurant Honmura An, noted for its handmade soba noodles, he spoke of his precise, permanently pleated fabrics, saying that the Japanese like things that are formed—paper origami, sweet bean cakes molded like flowers, sushi and textured fabrics, even as streams of blond noodles much like his pleats were hanging in the kitchen just behind him. Not long after I pointed that out, his shop on Madison Avenue had a window with noodles as the backdrop for his pleats. Expressing a taste for foods of his childhood, Issey said that although he flies out of Japan on many different airlines, he always goes back to Tokyo on Japan Airlines because they serve curry rice, a subsistence level, Indian-inspired dish popular during the impoverished days following World War II, and therefore a comforting retro relic.

Gianfranco Ferré, who creates layered costumes and studied architecture, preferred dishes that are multilayered, such as a huge boned turkey, stuffed with a boned capon, stuffed with a boned chicken and right on down to a tiny quail, all to be cut through for serving in tiered slices, a sort of poultry birthday cake, dating back to the Renaissance. Karl Lagerfeld, of German-Swedish descent, told me that he avoided French restaurants in Paris because they were dirty. The year I interviewed Yves Saint Laurent in his Left Bank apartment, he was eating only white food, pale pink ham being the only exception.

Of the twenty or so such interviews I did, two stand out above the others, one with Muhammad Ali and the other with Saul Bellow and his friend and colleague Allan Bloom. The most amazing thing about Ali was the man himself, his leopard-like stalk-walk, his size and equally monumental presence that made me feel as though I was indeed with a superhuman, perhaps from another planet. I still recall shaking his outsize hand and noting its pleasantly dry, almost grainy skin. We met at the Concord Hotel in Kiamesha Lake in upper New York State, where he was in training for a fight with Ken Norton. I spent two days with his cook, Lana Shabazz, sampling the dishes that were his favorites—spiced lamb shanks, Muslim bean soup, baked okra and tomatoes and carrot cake, while the ex-comedian Dick Gregory took care of the vitamin department by swirling up Champ Juice (citrus juices with maple syrup and spring water). Lana Shabazz also made sure that all rules of the Muslim diet were observed—no sweet potatoes (but butternut squash was all right), no gaseous vegetables of the cabbage family, collards included, no watermelon and very few white starches.

Following the Muslim diet, Ali announced, "Norton eats pork and he is pork. I do not eat pork and I am not pork. That's why I am going to win. A man is what he eats." He added that Norton would lose also because he ate women.

On hearing from my then agent, Harriet Wasserman, that Saul Bellow, another of her clients, liked to eat and sometimes to cook, I asked her to arrange an interview. We met for lunch in the small, darkish campus apartment of Allan Bloom, Bellow's colleague at the Committee on Social Thought at the University of Chicago. Tall, softly fat and loose-jointed, Bloom, who stammered, had a sensuous face reminiscent of that of the British actor Robert Morley, with thick lips that always seemed to be wet, as though he had just been eating, and a sense of humor strangely Jewish for someone so devoted to the classics. Bellow could not have seemed more opposite, with his lean, compact build and impeccable dress that reminded me of a raffish tap dancer. From that meeting on we were friends, and both Allan and Saul, first with his wife Alexandra and later with Janis when they married, served as the Chicago branch of the Green Beret eaters whenever I was there reviewing. They never were recognized, once much to Bellow's annoyance when as we were leaving, a waitress said to him, "I hope you enjoy your stay in Chicago," to which he replied, "I have lived here most of my life." Later he bridled, saying that he would have been recognized at any café in Paris, but nowhere in Chicago, because, he said, as he had before, "Here the philistines are really philistines."

The first lunch began with a mushroom and barley soup made by Bloom himself and was something of a specialty, he bragged. Saul brought the leanest corned beef I have ever seen from a deli he wanted to keep secret, "but it's in East Rogers Park," he added teasingly. He need not have worried about me, as leanness in corned beef has never seemed the prize. But lean the Nobel laureate was about everything, including his hatred of greasy pots that prompted him to wash all of them himself at home. He felt no one else would get them so clean and warned against using steel wool or scouring powders for the task because one leaves little threads in the grooves of the pot while the other leaves powder. He soaked them in hot soapy water, then cleaned them with a rough cloth. Explaining his method for preparing beef stew, Bellow said he added some soy sauce, curry powder and ginger, at which point Bloom said, "I always liked that stew but I never knew those things were in it." Bellow said he was not surprised because Bloom was "taste blind."

A few days after the story appeared, Harriet Wasserman told me that Bloom was hurt and upset, for though I mentioned his mushroom and barley soup, I did not say whether I had liked it. Alas for him if I had. He had used far too many carrots, causing the soup to look orange-stained and taste overly sweet. Neither of us ever mentioned the soup when we met.

On an evening when we had dinner at a highly overrated and pretentious Chicago restaurant, Bellow commented, "I see the nouvelle, but where's the cuisine?"

Some years later, when Bloom had great financial success with his book *The Closing of the American Mind*, he invited me to dinner at his new apartment with Saul, Janis and my son, Marc, who was then at the University of Chicago law school. It was a huge, bright apartment with a gigantic sound system filling an entire room, and the dining room table was profusely set with Hermès toucan-patterned china. We were invited there to try the food of a young Asian chef whom Bloom was mentoring—Michael Wu, the inspiration for the character Nikki in Bellow's thinly disguised novel about Bloom, *Ravelstein*. What Bloom/Ravelstein and Bellow/Chickie asked me to do for Michael/Nikki was to write a note stating his great ability as a chef to be presented to immigration authorities so that the young cook could get a green card. I did and he did.

Season to Taste

"**I**'D LIKE TO TAKE A DANCE CLASS, but I think I ought to take cooking lessons instead," a young secretary to one of my editors confided in me years ago, seeking guidance. I suggested she choose the dance because she seemed to regard that as pleasure and cooking as a duty. Taking cooking lessons reluctantly seemed the wrong way to start, as people who don't really like to cook will rarely be good at it, although they may have to learn a minimum for survival. That minimum is decreasing rapidly as more shops, supermarkets and restaurants offer a wide variety of take-out foods that are often relatively inexpensive. More and more, cooking is left to those who enjoy it when they have the time.

As much as I enjoy cooking, those who do not are in no way derelict or less valuable human beings. I just hope that when they invite me to dinner, they order out from the best possible source. It is being together and sharing good food and good talk that counts, no matter who prepares the meal. In recent years various groups advocating a return to traditional home cooking often take a moralistic tone, suggesting that anyone who does not want to spend time in the kitchen is somehow inferior, a view I do not share. Some of my best friends detest cooking and several are not at all interested in food, leaving us about ten thousand other engaging subjects to discuss.

My passion for food began with cooking and I am not at all sure that it was solely my mother's emphasis on it that influenced me. I might just as easily have rebelled, and if I did not, it was probably because something in me enjoyed handling food and pleasing people from the start and I was soon considered good at it, reinforcing my interest. Most of all, I like to prepare big, traditional meals for holidays, or ethnic foods for casual dinner parties at which eight guests is my preference though we often have ten, or for large parties, as on New Year's Day when about seventy guests come and go, sharing in an authentic smorgasbord based on recipes I gathered from Denmark and Sweden during the years I wrote about furniture design. Although such large parties require more work, they are somewhat simpler because I rarely have to worry about guests with food allergies or great dislikes, there being so much on such a buffet that they can choose from. For smaller dinner parties, I ask first-time guests in advance if they really hate a particular food (eggplant and mushrooms are frequently named) or if they have an allergy such as to nuts, and therefore, also to nut oil in salads or nut pastes in desserts. There are so many dishes I can prepare that it seems a pity not to adjust to a guest so that all will have a good time. I learned, however, that offering choices can go too far, as at one dinner for eight when I asked who would like coffee. Three said yes, two asked for decaf, one for tea, the next for decaffeinated tea and yet another for herbal tea, meaning five beverages for eight people. Coffee or tea, both with caffeine were the final choices, although I have since switched to decaffeinated coffee for all guests, even though I consider that solution inhospitable.

Less ambitiously, my idea of relaxation after a hard day at the computer is to make a potful of soup from things I find in the refrigerator and pantry. I usually stack the deck by including among staples carrots, celery, parsley, onions, garlic, cans of tomatoes and a fairly decent chicken stock (Health Valley Fat-Free Chicken Broth), rice and barley, split peas or lentils, Goya's canned white cannelini beans and often dried Polish mushrooms. Whether to use butter or olive oil, lemon or wine vinegar or to puree or not allows myriad permutations of the dish. Making soup allows me to keep my options open as long as possible, deciding whether to add milk or cream, or to puree for elegance or not for lustiness.

Braising, cooking by the slow, wet simmering method, also allows for impromptu variations. Although I broil, poach and sauté on ordinary nights when we dine at home, because those methods are quick and can be done lightly, the results are devoid of excitement compared to the long, languid process of developing stews, pot roasts, chicken and game birds that allow for exchanges of flavors among meat, herbs and spices, garlic and onions, each ingredient giving up a part of itself to create a totally new whole. Braising also appeals to me because it allows for maximum flavor with a minimum of intricate handwork that I am too impatient to do. By the time those fragrant stews, stracottos, sauerbratens, carbonnades and daubes are ready to serve, they have become part of my life, as I watch over them, tasting, basting and turning gently, sniffing the subtle changes in aromas as the magic progresses. Rich scents of wine and caramelizing meats and vegetables start mouths watering hours before the meal, preparing both palate and psyche for the main event. It is almost a sacred process that prompts me to leave a light on in the kitchen so that bubbling pots are never alone in the dark when I am elsewhere in the house. I regard that as real cooking, compared to the California grill-and-stack method by which foods are seared separately and so exchange no flavors before being combined in elaborate, towering arrays that substitute eye appeal for taste. It is a presentation I find aesthetically offensive because the intent is to make something very simple look complicated and is the very opposite of the accolade "seamless" that indicates a performer so skillful, he or she makes a difficult task appear easy. Among such performers are Sinatra, Matisse, Balenciaga and Antoine Magnin at Chez L'Ami Louis.

To love cooking is also to enjoy tangential activities, including collecting tableware and utensils. Although I shun cutesy gadgets and insubstantial amateur housewares and rely on a Garland range but have no microwave or toaster ovens, I am always carried away with the serious professional alternatives. My closets and basement are filled not only with hundreds of dishes in varying designs but with forms, molds, turbot poachers, pudding basins and such highly specialized ware as a set of flat, round, covered tins meant to mold ice cream into layers for a frozen cake. Having purchased those about forty years ago at Silber-Herthel, then a well-known restaurant supply house in Hamburg, Germany, I have yet to use them but expect to any day now, perhaps as soon as I finish writing this book. And as for the copperware, cutlery, charlotte molds, gratins and terrines purchased through the years at E. Dehillerin in Paris, don't ask.

Esoteric pieces that I have used include the wooden press for making *rullepølse* (the Danish rolled and spiced pork or veal sausage that is sliced thinly as an appetizer), the tall forms for the Russian Easter pashka (a fruit- and nut-studded cheese spread) and kulich (a sweet yeast coffee cake), an authentic *chittara* (the guitar-like pasta cutter used in the Abruzzi) and a Portuguese *cataplana* (the hinged, double round pot for making the spicy clam and sausage dish of the same name, although I have found other uses). I collect antique chocolate molds for their craftsmanship, history and symbolism purely as a hobby, and also because I would never be tempted to use them, not liking candy enough to bother.

As an adjunct to cooking, I look forward to shopping for food, especially at small ethnic shops that allow for entertaining conversations, and in farmers' markets such as the Union Square Greenmarket in Manhattan, which has become a meeting place for so many of the city's food professionals on Saturday mornings. Loving the life, color, drama and abundance of markets. I wrote about many in *Food Markets of the World*. My favorites in this country include the dazzling Ferry Plaza Farmers' Market in San Francisco, the arty Wednesday and Saturday event in Santa Monica, the Saturday produce stalls rimming Marion Square in Charleston that suggest a country fair, and the twenty-three-acre Green Dragon market held on Fridays in Ephrata, Pennsylvania.

Connoisseurship has its rewards, as in the successful selection of a perfectly ripe honeydew melon (an unblemished oval with a buttery-yellow rind that has a matte finish and feels sticky to the bare hand, indicating that sugar has risen to the surface) or a truly fresh fish that is bright of eye and blood, with a sweet sea smell and flesh supple enough to spring back when pressed. For anyone who knows how to cook without checking basic recipes, it is an adventure to build menus based on the day's most alluring offerings. I've always felt that spontaneity is what lends passion to Paris street markets, especially close to mealtimes, when shoppers make impromptu choices, rather than coldly plan what they will eat two or three days ahead, giving evidence of the old adage that there is no sauce like hunger.

In general, dishes that demand many ingredients are more exciting to shop for, none more so for me than a midsummer ratatouille with vegetables that offers as much tactile pleasure and appeals to palate and eye. Rarely are there more beautiful edible forms—the gleaming dark purple-brown globes of eggplant, gray-green lengths of zucchini, glossy emerald green peppers, and the crimsons of ripe sweet peppers and tomatoes, the subtle sheen of garnet-colored onions and forest bouquets of parsley and basil accented, visually and gustatorily, by paper-white garlic heads. Having long had a passion for still-life paintings of food, and always wondering how the ingredients shown might work into a particular dish or meal, I arrange the vegetables of ratatouille on a marble counter in a way I claim is haphazard, but is not quite.

Every step of preparation—cutting, layering, simmering—brings sensual pleasure from the colors and aromas that add up to the very essence of Provence. For the same reasons, I delight in preparing mixed fish soups and stews such as bouillabaisse or zuppa di pesce—all with the sort of crustaceans, mollusks and whole fish that inspired Dutch *stilleven*.

Although I do not believe one has to know how to cook to be a reliable restaurant critic, the knowledge certainly helps a critic to describe food convincingly and explain where it fails or succeeds. It is, however, no more necessary to cook well than for a drama, dance or art critic to perform or paint. It is essential to have a standard for a particular dish, based on an example the critic has liked best, and to know what ingredients the dish should contain. To write that a roast was burned, dry or overdone is sufficient without explaining what the oven temperature should have been, or that the meat was insufficiently basted or that the wrong cut of meat was used. On the other hand, if ingredients in a dish differ from the classics, the critic should know enough to say so and then decide if the switch is acceptable or, perhaps, even preferable. A coq au vin made with white wine instead of the classic red might appeal and cast new light on that dish, but a critic should be aware that white is a substitution. Very few writers have described food and restaurants so well and accurately as A. J. Liebling. When I once asked his wife, the writer

Jean Stafford, if he could cook, she said not really, other than scrambled eggs or an omelet now and then, but that he knew how many dishes should be prepared and was especially good at telling new kitchen help exactly how to cook a perfect rack of lamb.

Obviously a food critic should be able to identify ingredients in a dish accurately, although exact flavors may be elusive due to overly complex combinations or obscuring presentations. I recall one such instance when Dick and I were having dinner in Santa Barbara with Julia Child at the restaurant Norbert's, and her boneless duck breast arrived sliced paper thin. Remarking that she would have preferred the whole breast so she could cut it as she liked and enjoy more texture, Julia observed that it can be hard to tell duck from lamb when cut that way, something I, too, had noticed on occasion.

My ability to identify what I was eating reached its peak one evening when I was reviewing the Japanese noodle soup restaurant Omen in New York's SoHo. We were six altogether, Dick and I with Marc and another couple with their daughter. We shared a number of small dishes before trying the soups and because the two teenagers were ravenous, offerings on the tiny plates disappeared faster than you could say sayonara. Still hungry, I spotted what looked like shaved white daikon radish in soy sauce. Reaching over with chopsticks, I snared the mound and began to eat it when I noticed something strange. "This tastes like paper soaked in soy sauce," I announced. Looking up, Dick said, "You are eating my napkin!"

Other requirements for a food critic are a hearty appetite, a cast-iron stomach, good health with no food allergies, a high metabolism and broad firsthand experiences with many cuisines, a good and unprejudiced palate and a dependable taste memory. Then comes the really hard part: the ability to write clearly and engagingly. All make for a combination of talents that is very hard to find, and editors have great difficulty in filling such openings, just as they do for writer-specialists in any field, be it fashion, home furnishings, finance, science, sports or the arts.

"Is cooking an art?" I am often asked, to which I answer no, not in the strictest sense, because it is done to fulfill a function—satiate hunger and maintain life. In much the same way, I do not consider architecture an art, because its primary purpose is to shelter people and their activities without falling down. I ascribe to the philosophy that true fine art is its own—and only—excuse for being. If anything, there are elements of the performing arts in cooking, in that a dish has to be rendered anew each time it is to be experienced and so always varies within limits, and also in that the recipe takes the place of a score, a script or a choreograph. As with fashion and interior design, architecture and other activities, food preparation requires artfulness and artistry.

Craft and science are two basic skills absolutely required of the cook. Craft is what most amateur cooks rarely master—they skip over cutting and chopping skills, never learn how to properly brown meat, or to stitch closed the cavity of poultry that is stuffed, or to judge by sight, smell, touch and even sound if something is cooking at too high a heat, is about to burn or is, perhaps, idling and not cooking at all. Just as a carpenter has to know which wood to choose for a particular purpose and what tool to work it with, so mastering the craft of cookery means knowing which utensils to use and also how to select the ingredients. Which variety of apple is best for pie as compared to one that is best for baked apples or applesauce? Has a careless butcher carving out a particular cut of meat unknowingly sliced through to an adjoining section that demands a different method of cooking? Such a mistake will result, for example, in a pot roast that is tender and juicy on one side, but rubbery on the other. Oddly, the craft flaw I most often find is in detecting staleness of meat that has darkened and taken on the faint odor of putrefaction, or of fish that was frozen, thawed and sold as fresh, or of over-the-hill pre-cut cheese smelling of ammonia or, most commonly perhaps, of oil-rich nuts and seeds that have turned rancid, even in the products of professional bakers. There may even be those who like the flavor of rancidity, considering it authentic to poppy seeds and walnuts.

Science plays a large part in cookery as well, and even those of us who have no idea about the principles of chemistry and physics involved have learned scientific dos and don'ts. We add baking powder to cause a cake to rise. We beat air into egg whites until they're stiff and shiny so they will expand when heated without breaking, thus uplifting a soufflé. Knowing cooks do not use pots made of reactive metals for cooking egg- or wine-based white sauces or acidic vegetables such as spinach, nor do they heat milk with lemon juice (unless they want a curdled near-cheese) or add too much oil to the beaten egg yolks for mayonnaise (lest the emulsion break). When I feel the need to know the science behind a process, I read *On Food and Cooking* by Harold McGee for answers that are both clear and informative.

To me, artistry in cooking relates to seasonings and is the most difficult element to master. (It has nothing to do with plate arrangement, which is basically a design skill and interests me the least.) Anyone who tries can learn culinary craft and science, and perhaps even improve a sense of taste through experience, but no amount of work and dedication will ever make a great cook out of one who has a poor or undiscerning palate. I am often served impeccable-looking food in restaurants and homes, perfectly cut, cooked and arranged, only to find it bland or downright awful on the palate. It is much the same as a serious, dedicated and uncompromising painter who has a bad eye and so is a failed artist.

Flavor is what interests me most as a cook when I try to match or improve upon previous versions of a dish I am preparing—always working toward a definite taste result that I have in mind. To get that result, I taste most of the ingredients I work with and in progressive stages of preparation. How acidic, sweet or watery are the fresh or canned tomatoes? How are they developing in the sauce? Is the basil a sort of mint and parsley blend as expected or has it taken on a musky undertone as mine from the garden does in late summer? Butter, oil, vinegar, wine, spices, prepared mustards and parsley are all ingredients that require checking so the cook knows what he or she is dealing with and can adjust. I do not taste raw meat or poultry although I sniff and poke it and begin to nibble as soon as it has some heat. Not to taste while cooking is much like choosing a color scheme with closed eyes.

"Season to taste," then, is arguably the most important phrase in the culinary vocabulary, fraught with as many hazards as "bombs away" or "fire when ready." It is a phrase glibly used by writers of recipes, myself included, partly to cop out on the exact seasonings required, but more positively, to let the cook modify the particular ingredients being worked with and, of course, attune them to his or her own palate. And there's the rub. For what pleases one palate might disgust another and there is always the critical question "Whose taste and compared to what?" As a critic I sometimes wonder if my opinions are valid for those under thirty, many of whom have had totally different taste experiences from mine. I may bemoan the absence of authentic French pâté de campagne, the dense cold meatloaf heady with garlic, cognac and bay leaves, but a hip downtowner of twenty-five might consider it too heavy, fatty, salty and who knows what else. Sooner or later, though, the reassuring recollection will come to me that although I grew up almost solely on American, Cantonese and Eastern European Jewish cookery, it was love at first bite in my virgin samplings of escargots, moules marinière, spaghetti amatriciana, paella and a wide world of other choices, all far removed from the taste paradigms of my childhood.

I was never more aware of taste being a matter of habit than when sampling the much-lauded all-natural, unaged beef of Argentina that is grass fed, lean and hormone free. Never have I so much wanted to like something and never was I so conflicted by my findings. The quest began at Beacon, the New York restaurant known for its skillful wood-oven roasting and where both Argentinian and American beefsteaks were on the menu. Comparing them, I decided that I preferred the American steaks for their unctuously fatty texture and more intense, aged flavor. "That's only because you're used to it," said Waldy Malouf, Beacon's accomplished chef, unaware that he had flung a gauntlet. To double-check, I also went to the excellent Chimichurri Grill on New York's Ninth Avenue, where my reaction to the beef remained the same even as I was beguiled by chef Jorge Rodriguez's cushiony, meat-filled empanadas, his Argentinian-Italian agnolotti and his frothy mushroom cappuccino soup.

Having already planned a trip to Buenos Aires to interview an eighty-three-year-old former bialy baker for *The Bialy Eaters*, I allotted more time to learn what I could about Argentinian beef (thereby getting my palate used to it), a subject I was assigned to write about for the *New Yorker*. For two weeks Dick and I visited *estancias*, the ranches where various breeds of cattle came eye to eye with us through automobile windows and where a few guilty minutes later we sampled cuts of their relatives at *asados* (meat roasts) done over *parrilla* grills in the countryside. One morning we climbed across catwalks suspended above all-too-fragrant livestock pens in the city's stockyards to watch the seven A.M. auctions. Ensconced in the old world comfort of the Alvear Palace Hotel, we made reservations at restaurants of every class, where we sampled all cuts of the famed beef. Although Dick liked it more than I did, I watched as he often and uncharacteristically reached for salt. Beguiled by the appetizers—a parade of delectable grilled beef innards such as sweetbreads, tongue, heart, liver, kidneys and blood sausage—I nevertheless kept missing flavor heft in the steaks even in the *chorizo* (sirloin) cut that I thought the best. I wondered if blandness accounted for the local custom of serving the meat with the pungent green herb, garlic and chili chimichurri sauce. In the end, I was so conflicted that I never wrote the story, feeling that in order for it to be valid, I should be able to take a stand.

We critics use the word good—or even wonderful—when we really mean that we like—or love—a particular dish. Taste, however, is a matter of experience that varies widely with age, ethnic background, locale and era, and when someone tells me he or she disagrees with me and likes a restaurant that I hate, all I can say is, "By all means eat there and enjoy." Even the Supreme Court has ruled that there is no such thing as a wrong opinion, or, therefore, no right one, either.

Although I wrestle with all of the above concerns intermittently, I have never let them color my reviews, which I write in the traditional, practical way, knowing that if many disagreed with my assessments I would not be paid to make them for long. That means there is a large enough audience ascribing to the same flavor standards as I do. That is why I always prefer the opinion of one reliable expert whose standards I am familiar with rather than a consumer consensus in which I cannot tell who has been influenced by whom and if there is any really informed opinion weighing in. To follow that course is to agree that McDonald's offers the world's best hamburger, for certainly it is the most popular.

If in the deepest dark of night I had any doubts about rendering taste verdicts for others, they were nothing compared to those that began to haunt me when I heard about the work of Dr. Linda M. Bartoshuk, while I was at *Time*. Dr. Bartoshuk, a psychophysicist, holds forth at the Yale University School of Medicine, where she is part of the otolaryngology (ear, nose and throat) department. Her work on taste, along with that of colleagues concerned with sound and smell, relates to measuring sensory perceptions both qualitatively and quantitatively, mostly for neurological diagnoses and only incidentally for consultations with industry. The words she uttered that intrigued me were, "No two palates are alike. We each live in a very different taste world."

Working in a laboratory using chemical solutions to activate the four areas on the tongue that account for all of the flavors we experience—sweet, sour, bitter and salty—Dr. Bartoshuk measures the ability to identify a flavor and determine its strength so that she can measure a subject's sensitivity.

"For example, it is possible that a person with low sensitivity for the sweet taste would require twice as much sugar to perceive a given level of intensity for that taste," she explained. "We also wonder if people who claim to like extremely bitter foods are really expressing a hedonic or pleasure preference for bitter or are simply taste-blind to it," she went on, adding that such traits are genetic.

From the first moment I heard about her experiments, I was determined to take part in one and she generously complied, providing material for a *Time* article. Would I prove to be a supertaster of bitter or sweet and so report on broccoli di rape and chocolate mousse in a way not valid for the normal tasters among my readers? Or would I be an undertaster (having a high taste threshold) of salt or sour, thereby leading the innocent astray?

For ninety minutes I sat with my tongue hanging out over a trough so it could receive the chemical solutions that would wash across it from tubes. It was interesting to note how the flavors "felt." Salt and sweet seemed warm and pleasant with sweet the more relaxing and salt the more exhilarating. Bitter curled the edges and sour felt icy and caused the surface of the tongue to contract. Next, for a "whole mouth" test, I rinsed with a diluted solution and wore headphones into which sounds were piped, my task being to relate the strength of the taste sensation to that of the sound, a procedure known as magnitude matching. In theory, if all other things are normal, one's sensory perceptions should match in intensity, all deteriorating comparably after age fifty, alas. If taking I.Q. tests prompted forebodings when I was in elementary school, this taste I.Q. terrified me as a food critic.

Fortunately I need not have worried, having tested very high on the qualitative aspects—identifying flavors at the lowest levels of concentration, partly due to naturally low thresholds but also to my training as a taster. I turned out to be a strong (but not super) taster of the two bitter stimuli (phenylthiocarbamide, or PTC, and propylthiouracil, or PROP), and because I could taste them at the weakest stimulating solutions, Dr. Bartoshuk concluded that I probably had two dominant genes for bitter tasting. Who knew?

Back in Manhattan, I went straight to Lutèce, there to exercise my quantitative and qualitative abilities. Salt was perfection in André Soltner's escargots en brioche, and my sweet threshold was crossed gently by the caramelized onions in the Alsatian tart. The sour and bitter sections of my tongue rejoiced at the harmony in the house-cured choucroute and my bittersweet predilections were met in chocolate mousse.

Still, whenever Dick raves about some very strong broccoli di rape that I think tastes medicinal, I say to myself, "It's bitter for me. Why isn't it bitter for you?"

Eating My Words

L OOKING BACK over a half century of writing about food, I naturally reflect on the many changes that have taken place in the products and restaurants we can choose from as well as in home cooking and the public's perception and attitudes concerning all of these. Nothing is what it used to be, for better or for worse (myself included), but most things still are relatively the way they were.

Being of a certain age, I wonder what other roads I might have taken. I always regret not having traveled the one leading to medical research and, with luck, to a cure for some dreaded illness. Other daydreams of might-have-been careers include art history, archaeology and antique textiles, subjects that have interested me along the way. Given my loathing of repetition, however, my sense is that I would have wound up writing about rather than practicing in any of those fields, with the exception of medical research.

What I have never considered, not even for a single moment, is owning a restaurant. Talk about repetition! Even worse, I would have to be in one place almost all of the time, catering to individual whims and personalities of customers. Had I been forced to earn a living in some other aspect of food, it might have been as the owner of a small take-out food shop where, once prepared, the dishes stay put and do not constantly have to be re-created. As another possibility, Dick and I have speculated on hiring ourselves out as a couple to a family of unlimited means. Being a superb driver, Dick could be the chauffeur and I would cook while we enjoyed a carefree existence in our love nest over the garage, never mind the carbon monoxide fumes from below. Naturally, we would be wired while on duty and take notes for the book that would surely be forthcoming, cook and chauffeur diaries having far greater possibilities than even those of a nanny.

As a former critic, I feel no qualms nor do I have second thoughts about having given high-profile products and restaurants negative reviews, as I believe that only those make the positive ratings credible. At most, I regretted *having* to give such negative reviews, or even slightly reducing the rating of a usually superb restaurant such as Lutèce during one of its less masterful periods, when I took away one of four stars, to be returned two years later when the kitchen had snapped back into shape. I doubt that any rating I gave, no matter how negative, ever closed a restaurant unless it was pretty far gone anyway. (If I knew it was on the skids, I did not review it at all.) In fact, more restaurants receiving high ratings have closed than those that were poorly or modestly rated. Many are critic proof anyway, catering to a clientele that doesn't read reviews or care what they say, foremost among them being the bygone Mamma Leone's and now Tavern on the Green. A rave review might jam them up for a while, but a negative one would barely touch them.

One only has to consider the comparatively quick closings of *New York Times* four-star restaurants such as Jean-Georges Vongerichten's Lafayette in what is now the Swissôtel (formerly the Drake) and Lespinasse in the St. Regis Hotel, where Christian Delouvrier turned out exquisite food, to know that a high rating may not be a magic bullet for more than three months. You can lead the public to water, but if they don't like the look of a place or its location within a hotel, you can't make them drink—or eat.

What did give me pause was a loyal clientele's defection from a restaurant after it received a bad review. I only barely understood why my opinion should matter to those who had liked it so much in the past. Perhaps it was because they were embarrassed to invite guests, or suggest a business meeting at a place that had just been panned.

It has intermittently been suggested (by restaurateurs who have had bad reviews, naturally) that food critics should be trained and certified, while some critics themselves have tried to start organizations that define standards. I reject both notions because restaurateurs are not themselves certified other than for health permits and liquor licenses, and they are not required to know shiitake from Shinola, as many do not. The organization of critics would foster orthodoxy, something I detest, and would keep restaurant owners from getting an even break, one aspect being more important to a given critic than another. It has also been suggested that we need no food critics at all, but I think that if we all stopped writing for six months, there would be a sharp decline in restaurant business, our tangential service being to create controversy that makes readers interested in something they never cared about, and thereby create a market.

Minor regrets after twenty years away from the *New York Times* have to do with few people inviting us home to dinner and those who do generally making embarrassingly abject apologies for what they will serve, putting pressure on me to seem pleased. Even more regrettable and awkward is that when dining out with our friends, some still expect me to pay the check.

On a professional level, perhaps the biggest and most dramatic change I have seen is in the enormous variety of foods we now can choose from not only in so-called gourmet markets but, increasingly, in mainstream supermarkets, especially in large cities. Fifty or even thirty years ago, the white champignon was the only fresh mushroom available, whereas now there are often between six and twelve to choose from depending upon season—morels, chanterelles, porcini, cremini, oysters, portobellos, hedgehogs, enoki and more. Lettuces were represented in even the best greengrocers solely by iceberg, romaine, endive, bibb and Boston, and in Italian neighborhoods, also by escarole, arugula and chicory. Now salad possibilities usually include two types of radicchio, oakleaf and other red and green leaf lettuces, tatsoi, mizuna, frisée and many of those also in delicately tender baby versions. Much the same is true of cheeses, breads, oils, vinegars, coffees and teas, fish, meats, grains and more.

This embarrassment of choice is the result of consumer demand because of wider travel, mass communications via newspapers and television and the practical possibility of rapid transportation so that perishables can travel farther safely and quickly. Home cooks also have been made aware of exotic products by highly touted chefs whose triumphs were widely covered by the press, creating culinary awareness and affording cooks an opportunity to taste something brand-new in a restaurant before having to cope with it at home.

What also has changed is the public perception of freshness as an aspect of gourmandise. In 1972, when I wrote "I Tasted Everything in Bloomingdale's Food Department" for *New York*, a project that took eleven months and the sampling of 1,196 individual items, Bloomingdale's was the fanciest, most prestigious grocery store in town. Like so many others then in the gourmet category, the department's majority of stock featured cans of expensive "delicacies" such as sauces including the delicate béarnaise and Newburg, soups from all over the world and, the greatest travesties, perhaps, dozens of prepared main courses such as cooked scallops and shells for coquilles St. Jacques, *tripes à la mode de Caen* from France, Scottish haggis, Swedish meatballs in dill cream sauce, and truly disgusting English game birds such as grouse and pheasant with sodden, mudlike meat in dark brown sauces that tasted as if they had been laced with lighter fluid. Add to that the prestige of imported canned vegetables from France, Holland, Switzerland, Germany and Belgium, all considered so ultra fancy that toney restaurants were proud to dish them up undisguised. In 1978 when I reviewed the '21' Club in New York and called to confirm that the peas were canned, the director, Sheldon Tannen, said that they were not just canned peas. "They're French petits pois!" So I wrote that they were canned little peas.

In addition, fancy food departments in those days generally had no fresh produce, or fish and meat departments, although they did display cases of cheeses, sausages, pâtés and various smoked and cured fish and herrings. Fortunately, aesthetic standards have improved greatly, with more sophisticated audiences preferring a fresh local product to one that arrives canned, even from France, a great tribute to food writers, chefs and the burgeoning farmers' markets around the country. More soberingly, the term farmers' market is rapidly being co-opted by commercial interests offering standard agribusiness produce that may indeed come from a "farm," never mind how vast or industrialized.

Not too surprisingly, perhaps, there have been many losses

among the gains. As the audience for certain foods becomes wider, quality tends to decline, there never being enough of the best to go around. Also, purveyors seeking as wide an audience as possible temper flavors to appeal to the broadest possible market and so modify them. Thus we have jalapeño chilies that have lost their sting, fish markets featuring only yuppie choices such as shellfish and fillets (Ah, for a fillet of life, I often think . . .), honey-sweet golden pineapples with no acidic tingle and shelves full of unripe fruits that will never ripen, having been picked too soon so that they will travel well. And when have you last had a grape that tasted of white wine as those in Italy do? We have also lost many perishable varieties such as juicy local strawberries in favor of the long-lasting large hollow specimens grown in California, and the big orange *percoche*, the Italian cling peaches we used to get in August that tasted best when sliced and marinated for an hour or two in a full-bodied Italian red wine. Tot up as losses, too, Italian parsley now as tough as patent leather and huge wiry leaves of monster arugula, size and eye appeal being the prizes, while wrinkled ripeness in fruits, as in people, seems anathema to many Americans.

The most serious discussion of food products, however, must be reserved for our relatively new "frankenfoods," products that are being chemically and genetically manipulated, as well as others such as fish that are being farmed. No culinary Luddite, I believe that all of these things should be tried in the interests of increasing our food supply, most especially when related to protein, which so much of the world is literally dying to have. My apprehension relates only to how this will be done and whether the greed of the producers results in dangers to consumers or environment. I detest almost all farmed salmon that I have tasted and cooked, what with its intense fat and awful aroma when roasted or grilled, but I would

bet a lot that it is being produced responsibly and excellently somewhere in the world. I even have a good idea where, but I'm not
going to reveal it until I've had a chance to look.

I have never forgotten the admonition I read many years ago
written by Siegfreid Giedion, the Swiss social and architectural his-
torian who is best known for *Space, Time and Architecture*. In his
later book, *Mechanization Takes Command*, published in 1948, he
dealt with industrialization and its practical, physical, philosophical
and psychological effects on many aspects of life. In the chapter on
the mechanization of organic substances, namely bread and meat,
he warned:

> No field within the entire scope of mechanization is so
> sensitive to mishandling as that of nutrition. Here mecha-
> nization encounters the human organism (whose laws of
> health and disease are still incompletely known). The step
> from the sound to the unsound is nowhere so short as in the
> matter of diet.
>
> This is not always immediately perceptible. The ultimate
> effects cannot usually be foreseen. If man deviates too long
> from the constant of nature, his taste becomes slowly vitiated
> and his whole organism threatened. Unwittingly, he impairs
> judgment and instinct, without which balance is so easily lost.

Speaking of vitiated, I'll never forget how depressed I was at a
salmon farm in Maine, when the "farmer" said that although the
salmon is a fighting fish, each generation bred in tanks becomes
more docile. And what of the consumers of those fish?

As for restaurants, I am relieved not to be covering the current
scene, so charged is it with culinary one-upmanship, as chefs cook for
one another and the press, rather than for the clientele. As exhilarating and praiseworthy as creative cookery can be, and as encouraging

and diverting as it is to have so many new practitioners, much of the time I feel as if I am, indeed, eating my words or those of my colleagues. There has always been a certain fashion element to food (post–World War II it was gazpacho, guacamole, seafood crepes, beef Wellington and steak Diane among others) and hot restaurants ('21', the Colony, Voisin, Le Pavillon, Café Chauveron) hard to get into, at least for the hoi polloi, but starting with the invention of nouvelle cuisine in France in the mid-1960s and heating up to the present explosion of creative cooking, chefs have followed the examples of fashion designers and behave accordingly, with the willing and extravagant cooperation of the press. Just as a couturier must have three or four new lines a year with some bizarre specimens to wow them on the runway, so chefs now feel they must do likewise and for the same reason—to get attention. Just as fashion writers rarely report on classics such as black cashmere sweaters and white silk shirts, so food writers rarely report on perfect omelets or roasted chicken or meatloaf unless they are presented in some groundbreaking context, such as nouvelle down-home.

At best this trend has given us wonderful chefs and exciting new dishes and has attracted better educated and more conscientious practitioners, many of whom are Americans now enjoying the status formerly accorded only to the French or to those Swiss or Italian chefs who masqueraded as French. Once considered servants, chefs now can be celebrity superstars, a big step up that André Soltner attributes to the charismatic efforts of Paul Bocuse. Obviously that has a downside, as we see all too often when pride gives way to ego as a chef refuses to modify a dish to a guest's taste in minor ways, such as refusing to leave a certain herb or spice out when that is possible, or by charging extra for substitutions such as a vegetable for potatoes, or to me the most blatantly pretentious practice, not putting salt and pepper on the table. Then there is the

matter of the absentee chef off on a celebrity toot instead of staying home at the range. First we are asked to believe that such a
superstar has golden hands, then we are told it doesn't matter if
those hands are working the kitchen or not.

Since the advent of nouvelle cuisine, there has been a premium
on creativity with new dishes, the French critics Gault and Millau
having reserved their very top ratings only for those who practiced
the new cooking, thereby becoming advocates. Unfortunately, there
are more chefs—and more fashion designers—who are good at
reproducing the classics than there are those who are equally good
at inventing, but who might well pay heed to the remark made by
the architect Robert A. M. Stern: "It is better to be good than to be
original." Nowhere is wildly absurd creativity more misplaced
than in the preparation of food that we must swallow. Not even
fashion designers really expect anyone to buy or wear their most
outrageous creations and often they never actually produce them,
which makes me wonder if certain chefs really expect anyone to eat
their wildest creations or if they want to be judged by their goals
rather than by their achievements. Another celebrated architect,
Richard Meier, in an interview in *Time* many years ago, described
postmodernism as "the illiterate application of symbols." And so it
is with food these days as terminology is thrown around without
real meaning just to prove the chef has taken it into consideration.
In architecture such symbolic application might include, for example, a Chippendale broken pediment atop a purely modern stone
building, with perhaps an Ionic column or a Gothic arch here or
there. In a description of a dish, classic culinary terminology is
often invoked with words such as jus, ragout, mousse, salmis, civet
or infusion even when those preparations actually were not followed. With menus, as with architecture, the message to the public
is the same: you can trust the creator who is really with it and at the
same time acknowledges the classics by nodding toward them.

As emphasis on fusion cooking and the search for the most exotic, heretofore unheard-of ingredients increases, I believe many chefs are anticipating the press by devising dishes that "sound" good or "read" well. Then they work back to stir them up in a pot and, in effect, cook up our copy. Little else can explain a dish that might read "curried T-bone of halibut in a lemongrass-ponzu jus over Yukon potato and yuzu ravioli under a pomegranate syrup reduction circled by harissa-spiked savoy cabbage wontons infused with fennel pollen and huitlacoche." Talk about food for thought! Think of the message such a dish conveys. First, that you can enjoy healthful fish even though you prefer high-cholesterol beef because this cut is a T-bone that is, after all, a kind of steak. And if you doubt the chef's commitment to multicultural fusion, consider the ethnic mélange he sets before you: Indian, American, Thai, Japanese, Italian, Moroccan, Chinese and Mexican. It tells you almost everything you need to know, except how this all will go down. For that, the waiter will gladly recite explanations of yuzu, ponzu, harissa, fennel pollen and huitlacoche to the uninitiated, by which time you may feel as though you have had more than enough.

Oddly enough, most such inventions lead to depressing similarities, as I have found by going to one fusion restaurant after another, mostly because the less talented among chefs, always a majority, get their ideas by observing one another and responding to competitors' menus. The most brilliant and successful base their riffs on traditional culinary roots, whether their own or of a foreign cuisine that they diligently studied. Thus, to me the best creative fusion practitioners include Jean-Georges Vongerichten for his research into Thai and Chinese cooking that led to Vong, the Spice Market and 66; Jean-Marie Josselin at A Pacific Café on the Hawaiian island of Kaua'i, where his French-informed pan-Asian specialties include a sprightly wasabi beurre blanc; David Bouley and Kurt

Guttenbrunner for morphing classic Viennese cooking into the evolved but convincing specialties they dish up at Danube and Wallsé; and Ana Sortun, whose Mediterranean–Middle Eastern fare is so inspired and inspiring at Oleana in Cambridge. Similarly, modern ethnic cooking is most successful when based on classics and given a new look but plenty of that old-time flavor, as at Daniel Boulud's db Bistro Moderne and any place that Christian Delouvrier works his Gallic magic, just as Cesare Casella at Beppe and Mario Batali at Babbo do with Italian food or Douglas Rodriguez and Aaron Sanchez with evolved Latino fare.

Far less likely to be successful are chefs who do not have sharply defined culinary backgrounds to draw upon, one of the few brilliant exceptions being Wylie Dufresne at wd-50, where he turns out superb modern fusion specialties, on New York's Lower East Side.

The shibboleth making the rounds right now that bothers me is that French cuisine is finally irrelevant and that the excellence of about half a dozen Spanish chefs automatically wipes out the centuries-old French predominance. What is interesting is that such opinions are retailed with apparent glee as though to say, "Aha! At last! The French have met their comeuppance." Not that they don't deserve to in large measure, of course, but it would be a shame to throw the *bebe* away with the bathwater. Such assertions have been made in relation to the French influence on fashion for many years now, but the very writers who make them still return to Paris several times a year to see the shows, and France is still the point of reference and the benchmark as to the creativity and talent of non-French interlopers.

If French cuisine is so dead, why are all the five *New York Times* four-star restaurants French? Even my own favorite restaurant (since André Soltner left Lutèce) in this country is La Grenouille in New York, still unmatched for beauty, professionalism and exquisite food. The *quenelles de brochet* alone make a visit worthwhile.

Come to think of it, as much as I love Chinese, Japanese and Italian food, my favorite restaurant in the world for many years has been Chez L'Ami Louis in Paris. Not having been there in about five years, I can only hope that the giant escargots sizzling in their shells, the unctuous foie gras that is the best I ever have had, the roasted chicken, côte de boeuf and gigot of lamb with potatoes roasted in duck fat, and the civet of hare that is redolent of medieval history, are all as I remember them. Part of my affection for this dilapidated, insanely expensive bistro is due to my rediscovery of it in 1979, when, after hearing so much about the young turks of French cuisine, I wanted to find the oldest chef in Paris. He turned out to be Antoine Magnin, then eighty, at Chez L'Ami Louis. Although consistently successful, his restaurant was not much talked about after the '50s and '60s. The success of our dinner and of the resultant article convinced me that when everyone is looking to the right, it is time to turn my gaze left.

The one thing that does bother me about the term French food is what such food really consists of in today's postmodern context, when, for example, a spot called the Italian Bistro opens in New York and I wonder if a French Trattoria can be far behind. What, after all, is French about most pasta dishes, carpaccio, osso buco and other Italian dishes rampant on the menus of so-called French restaurants in America?

Midst all of this, I found myself longing for old-time French dishes, mostly at the bistro level but some distinctly haute. And so in the latter part of 2003 I began a project I titled "À la Recherche du Plats Perdus." In our search for lost dishes, Dick and I are eating our way through some seventy-five New York City restaurants seemingly French but are eliminating those with none or very few of the identifying items on their menus: escargots bourguignon, pâté de campagne, salade Lyonnaise, coquilles St. Jacques, *maquereau au vin blanc*, onion soup and soupe de poissons, sole meunière and goujonettes of sole, coq au vin, boeuf bourguignon, daube, cassoulet, choucroute garni, *canard aux navets, cuisses de grenouilles à la provençale, boeuf en ficelle, pieds de cochon à la St. Menehould, rognons rotis* and about a dozen more. Not that any one restaurant has to have all, but there must be a decent representation. That we have been through about thirty-five so far with only limited success has not dampened our spirits or our sense of purpose. Stay tuned . . .

While we can congratulate ourselves on the increasing diversity in restaurants around the country, some losses must be acknowledged. What I miss most are the many excellent and often elegant dining places that used to offer the best dishes of Germany and Scandinavia, both having fallen out of fashion due to images of heaviness and because many had deteriorated. Yet about forty years ago both were downright trendy, at least to serious food lovers who frequented German restaurants such as Luchow's, the Blaue Donau, Jaeger Haus and Café Geiger (known for extraordinary beef tartare that was scraped, not ground or chopped) in New York; the Golden Ox in Chicago, and Karl Ratzsch's and Mader's in Milwaukee. All featured elegant game, crisp schnitzels, wine-flavored sauerkraut, apple pancakes and more. Of that group only the two in Milwaukee remain, although I have not been to them in years. And though food was bland and heavy-handed at Knoll's Black Forest Inn in Santa Monica a few years ago, there was more than enough evidence that the same fare can be delectably prepared with a light touch as it is at Spago in Beverly Hills, where Wolfgang Puck introduced some of the authentic dishes of his Austrian childhood. His delicately burnished, meltingly tender goulash is so popular with his trendy, health-minded clientele that he sells about fifty pounds every two or three days. The success of more modern riffs on these cuisines at Wallsé and Danube in New York with luck may tempt the public's palate enough to inspire even more traditional representations.

Scandinavian fare was at its peak of popularity when the designs of those countries were also in vogue, and New York offered a wide choice with such places as Gripsholm (now Mr. Chow), Copenhagen on the site of Le Grenouille, Castleholm on West 57th Street and Finland House on East 50th Street near Madison Avenue. Kungsholm in Chicago and Skandia in Los Angeles were other cases in point where most uninitiates unfortunately resorted to the smorgasbord tables, never venturing to printed menus that listed more subtle fare such as dill-scented fish dishes, golden pea soups, mellow red cabbage and lingonberry-accented game.

Just as some women gather jewels that they contemplate occasionally to cheer themselves up, so I can unwrap memories of favorite meals, a far less fattening pursuit than eating them. Certainly one was prepared for my birthday many years ago by Alain Sailhac, then at Le Cirque. Dick and Marc wanted to surprise me with one of my most beloved arcane dishes, pheasant à la Souvarov, a rich combination of the game bird roasted with truffles, foie gras and Madeira after the lid of the casserole has been sealed hermetically with a stiff flour and water paste. Sailhac substituted a complete cover of pastry instead of using the lid, and as the huge red enameled casserole was rolled to our table, the entire dining room stared, then sniffed, as the crust was broken and the taunting aroma floated upward. As I recall, the first courses were artichokes Barigoule braised in olive oil with mushrooms, ham and a bit of tomato and garlic, followed by another Sailhac specialty, a cool salad of lobster meat bedded on the briny seaweed *pousse-pierre*.

Other French triumphs came at Le Français in Wheeling, Illinois, where Jean Banchet dished up his incomparable pâtés and charcuterie and his many dishes based on innards and game. Harking back to the test days for the Four Seasons, I was stunned and delighted to see a whole roasted calf's liver on the menu there one night. Banchet's had been baked in a pastry crust that was underlined with foie gras for what some might consider liver overkill, but not me.

Not all of my memorable meals have been fancy, one of the best being the New Orleans feast at Buster Holmes and another a lunch of a half-dozen roasted pigeons served with warm house-baked pita along the banks of the Nile in Cairo. There was also an exquisite private dinner given for me in the legendary antique Thai home (now a museum) in Bangkok of Jim Thompson, the architect who revived that country's silk industry after serving there in World War II. The sparkling sweet and pungent fried Thai noodles, *mee krob*, were followed by huge coral prawns grilled with garlic, sesame oil and a breath of lemongrass and klong spinach, a silky bittersweet green much like the springtime vegetable the Chinese call hong choy.

Confident that I have not yet had the best Italian and Chinese dinner of my life, I hope I have already had the two worst meals I will ever suffer. One was a lunch in the Umbrian town of Orvieto, where the day's special chicken arrived looking merely dead and wet with no color on a slippery, thick skin still strewn with hairy wisps of feathers. The other was a picnic Dick and I shopped for in Lincolnshire when we spent a month in England. Finding a pretty park and having a cold half bottle of white wine, we bit into a slice of meat pie and right through a layer of thick, cold, white fat that made me feel as though I was chewing a candle.

If my interest in food needed renewing at all, three things ensure that it will continue. One is a program I am working on with a few public high schools in New York, introducing food discussions to classes to inspire writing, reading and general cultural awareness. After only three such sessions at my alma mater, Midwood High School in Brooklyn, it is too soon to say how effective this will be, although some students already have started to write restaurant review columns for the school newspaper and some classes have held tastings about which they have written critiques.

Having repeatedly read my way through the works of M. F. K. Fisher, Elizabeth David, Joseph Wechsberg, Waverly Root and A. J. Liebling—the canon of writers that inspired my generation—I now am increasingly interested in the philosophical, psychological and spiritual symbolisms of various foods and eating customs. The first book to pique that interest was *The Lord's Table: The Meaning of Food in Early Judaism and Christianity* by Gillian Feeley-Harnik, in which the author, an anthropologist, describes all of the Old and New Testament admonitions concerning food and their meanings. Throughout there are promises of ample food and drink for the righteous and threats of drought and famine for sinners, with the heavenly banquet described (Isaiah 25:6–8) as a feast "of fat things full of marrow, of wine on the lees well refined." "To feed is to bless," observes the author, just as "to starve is to judge or punish." She also delves into the idea that by ingesting food according to biblical law is to ingest religious teachings, and that strict dietary prohibitions serve to keep a group intact, as members cannot easily socialize or intermarry with someone with whom they cannot break bread. It is a reminder that the word *companion* is derived from the Latin *com-panis*, "with bread."

In *The Hungry Soul, Eating and the Perfecting of Our Nature*, Dr. Leon R. Kass poses that all of our rules of eating, such as table etiquette, refined cookery and the proscribed orders of dishes in various cultures, are attempts to set ourselves apart—and above—other orders of animals by showing that we humans alone can control our most basic instincts. A neo-con member of The College of the University of Chicago's Committee on Social Thought and currently chairman of President Bush's council on bioethics, this medical doctor, despite his difficult prose, makes an intriguing case that started me on a whole new tack of observations of the way people eat and why.

Most inspiring of all, perhaps, is my granddaughter, Anna, who at a year and a half is beginning to try all sorts of new food, speculatively but hungrily. I have long felt that taste is the first aesthetic judgment made by a newborn and I have seen studies backing this up with photographs of facial expressions of infants after tasting sweet, sour and bitter. I carefully watch Anna as she picks up a new food, holds it in her mouth for a second or two with a faint troubled flicker across her brow and slightly pursed lips, and then either swallows it with a burst of glee or removes it from both mouth and plate and throws it on the floor. It is the sort of candid response I may adopt as my own restaurant behavior.

So far, she hasn't met a meatball she didn't like, whether her Italian great-grandmother's that are flavored with chopped parsley, Parmesan, garlic, grated lemon rind and tomato sauce, her Jewish great-grandmother's beef balls, soothingly accented with paprika and onions and braised in chicken fricassee, or the tiny clove- and allspice-scented Swedish *köttbullar* that attest to her grandmother's proselytizing for all things Scandinavian.

Apprehensive about the future, but content with the past, I have had a more marvelous life than I ever expected to, thanks to both my work and my family. There are two ways of measuring success: how far we have come from our beginnings, or how far we could have come. I am more than gratified by how far I have come. It remains to be seen how much further I will go.